black families and the struggle for survival

Andrew Billingsley
Study Questions and Guide
by Robert O. Dulin, Jr. and Edward L. Foggs

Published for The Committee on Ministries with Black
Families of the Black Christian Education Project
of the National Council of Churches.

FRIENDSHIP PRESS • NEW YORK

acknowledgments

The following credits express our appreciation to the writers and publishers who have allowed us to use their materials in this book.

Page 17, from *Selected Poems* by Langston Hughes. © 1959 by Alfred A. Knopf. Used by permission.

Page 38, reprinted from *The Redemption of Africa and Black Religion* by St. Clair Drake. Reprinted by permission of Third World Press, Chicago, Illinois.

Pages 44-45, from *Great Slave Narratives*, Arna Bontemps, ed. © 1969 by Beacon Press. Reprinted by permission of Beacon Press.

Pages 45-46, from *Black Slave Narratives,* edited and with an introduction by John F. Bayliss. © 1970 by Macmillan Publishing Co., Inc. Used by permission.

Page 51, from "The Black Family During Reconstruction", an essay by Robert Abzug in *Key Issues in the Afro-American Experiences,* Vol. II, edited by Nathan I. Huggins, Martin Kilson and Daniel M. Fox. Reprinted by permission of Harcourt Brace Jovanovich, Inc.

Pages 52-53, from *Black Families in White America* by Andrew Billingsley. © 1968. Reprinted by permission of Prentice-Hall, Inc.

Page 63, from *More Adventures of Spider* by Joyce Cooper Arkhurst. Used by permission of Scholastic Book Service.

Pages 63-64, from *A Quiet Place* by Rose Blue, copyright 1969 by the author. Used by permission of the publisher.

Page 67, from three songs by Ella Jenkins: "Play Your Instrument and Make a Pretty Sound", "You'll Sing a Song and I'll Sing a Song" and a song from "American Negro Folk and Work Song Rhythms." Used by permission of Ella Jenkins and Folkway Records.

Page 72, from *Bubbles* by Eloise Greenfield. Used by permission of Eloise Greenfield and Drum & Spear Press.

Library of Congress Cataloging in Publication Data

Billingsley, Andrew.
  Black families and the struggle for survival.

  "Published for the Committee on Ministries with Black Families of the Black Christian Education Project of the National Council of Churches."
  1. Negro families—United States. I. Title.
E185.86.B49   301.42'1   74-9839
ISBN 0-377-00001-9

Copyright © 1974 by Andrew Billingsley
Printed in the United States of America
Second Printing August 1977

A number of people have provided me assistance in the preparation of this volume. The Faculty Research Program in the Social Sciences, Humanities and Education at Howard University and the National Council of Churches provided financial assistance. For the initial idea, encouragement and support, I am grateful to George Thomas and Robert Dulin. I am also indebted to Marilyn Greene, who supervised the collection of data and the preparation of the preliminary and final reports. Jyllinda Hagler provided secretarial assistance. Members of my family, Amy, Angela and Bonita, provided invaluable support, suggestions and critical commentary. To these and the many others who inspired this work, and to all Black children and parents who teach each other how to walk tall, this books is affectionately dedicated.

This publication was made possible
by a grant from the
JOSEPH P. SUNNEN FOUNDATION
St. Louis, Missouri

contents

Foreword 7

1. Black Families in Perspective 11

2. We Are an African People 36

3. Slavery: The Americanization of the Africans 49

4. Teaching Our Children to Walk Tall 57

Notes 76

Study Guide 79
A Guide for Group Study and Discussion of *Black Families and the Struggle for Survival*

foreword

Numerous books and articles have been written about Black family life in America. Most of the literature available is academic and based upon research that evidences an incorrect analysis of the relationship between Black families and white society. It does not adequately deal with the relationships between Black families and the larger Black community. Most of the research published to date focuses upon one segment of the Black American community; namely, the lower class poor. Until very recently, the most popular understandings regarding the Black family were "myth" understandings identified with the inadequate conclusions of the "Moynihan Report" of 1965.

The "Moynihan Report" presented an image of the Black family in terms of its weaknesses and with little recognition or knowledge of the strengths of Black families. The Black family was viewed as a social problem ". . . incapable of perpetuating itself without assistance from the white world." In essence, "the deterioration of the Negro family" was seen as "the fundamental source of the weakness of the Negro community...." Following this line of reasoning the Black family was viewed as incapable of making a substantial contribution to its own community or to the nation. But thanks to the recent emergence of a cadre of Black scholars and researchers, the Moynihan perspective regarding the family life of Black people has undergone much criticism and refutation.

Unlike the literature that follows in the Moynihan tradition, the Committee on Ministries with Black Families of the Black Christian Education Project of the National Council of Churches contends with Andrew Billingsley and a host of other Black students of family life, "that Black families are among the strongest and most resilient institutions in the nation. Were it not so, we would not have survived as a people, and the national society would be even more inhuman and inhumane than it is." The very fact of the survival of Black families, despite a severely cruel system of slavery and oppression, is in itself prima facie evidence of the strength resident in Black families.

Thus, *Black Families and the Struggle for Survival* stands in contradistinction to those who see the structure of family life in the Black community as constituting a "tangle of pathology." Written in a very practical and popular style, this study attempts to assist a lay audience in identifying the strengths of Black families. The many complex factors that account for these strengths and that hinder their enrichment are identified and presented in ways that offer the church a constructive and promising challenge. Professional church persons and church lay leaders wishing to develop relevant and effective family-centered programs and ministries within the Black community will find this book most useful. It affords both helpful insights and tested resources for engaging churches and Black families in the common task of enhancing Black family life.

Where the church's ministry with families is concerned, this book confronts the reader with several important questions. For example:

(1) *What should be the goal of Black family life?*

(2) *How might the church go about assisting Black grandparents,*

parents, youth and children in the struggle of positive human development?

(3) Given the historical character of the Black family's existence and the continuing forces of disintegration, what should the Black church be about in terms of nurturing the strengths of Black families?

(4) Where should the Black family fit within the programmatic priorities of the church?

These are basic questions of concern regarding the work of the Committee on Ministries with Black Families. In this regard, the committee is pleased to work with Dr. Andrew Billingsley in making this resource available. In a skillful, readable and interesting way, Billingsley challenges us to extract from our history such details as will serve to enhance our appreciation for family life and the ways in which the authentic relationships of the extended family can contribute to the development of whole persons.

A study guide outlining ways in which this book might be used in the Black church's educational ministries with Black families is a part of this study text. In addition to the assistance this guide offers for using *Black Families and the Struggle for Survival,* it calls attention to a number of other relevant resources that might prove helpful to the leader in conducting study sessions based upon this text.

It is our hope that readers of this book will begin to sense the greatness of the challenge facing the Black church with respect to its constituent families. The urgency of this challenge becomes more significant when we reflect upon the possibility that the Black church and the Black family—in that order—might well be the last battleground of our struggle for survival. Writing with a similar concern in mind, the theologian J. Deotis Roberts has observed that our "task may seem more hopeful if we remember that the Black church was the family for Blacks when there was no organized family."

The Committee on Ministries with Black Families is indebted to Dr. Andrew Billingsley for making this literary contribution, challenging the church to begin shaping its ministries in ways that effect positive human development through the enhancement of healthy and authentic family relationships.

Robert O. Dulin, Jr.
Associate Minister for
   Educational and Family Ministries
   Metropolitan Church of God
   Detroit, Michigan
   and
Chairman of the Committee on
   Ministries with Black Families

Edward L. Foggs, Director
Urban Ministries
   Board of Church Extension and Home Missions of the Church of God (Anderson, Indiana)

February, 1974

1

black families in perspective

A family is generally considered to be a group of individuals related to each other by ancestry or marriage and living together in the same household. This is a fairly common definition of family. When we think of Black families, however, we are likely to think of a group of people of African heritage related to each other either by blood or marriage and who live together or who have lived together in the same household. It is evident that the standard definition of family is an inadequate description of our families. An important observation that should be made is that Black family life in America has many facets. It is not exactly like the family life of the dominant group. In some ways it is, and in some ways it is not. But in order to capture what we mean by Black families, it is more useful to think of people who are related, and people who feel that they themselves belong to each other. We must think of people who live together in the same house, and people who feel themselves to be closely related, but who live in different houses and often in different locations altogether. Furthermore, when we think of Black families, we must think of very strong bonds of kinship. For the concept of family, of belonging to the same closely related unit, is deeply ingrained in the Black experience.

Thus, whether we think of our African background, where family life was the central feature of community and national life; or whether we think of slavery, where even during that reign of terror many of our people held fast to the notion of belonging together even when separated; or whether we think of modern times, when the forces of racism, poverty and violence often keep us apart, the spirit of family is still strong among us. It has never died out. The family thus represents a most important aspect of the struggle of our people for survival. And, it has been the family more than any other institution which has helped our people to survive, to find meaning in life and to reach remarkable levels of achievement.

This study of Black family life in America is one approach to the set of hard questions we are asking ourselves these days; namely, "Who are we as a people?" "Where did we come from?" "Where are we going?" It is our view that Black families are among the strongest and most resilient institutions in the nation. Were it not so, we would not have survived as a people, and the national society would be even more inhuman and inhumane than it is.

This view is strikingly different from the more typical view of Black families that one finds in most literature. The typical view and analysis of research data begins with the idea and concludes with the opinion that Black families are weak, matriarchal, unstable and make no substantial contribution to Black people or the nation. Our view is just the opposite. It grows out of not only personal experience and observation, but also out of considerable research and analysis of the research of other scholars. Our view is most consistent with that of a relatively new stream of Black scholarship exhibited by such students of family life as Hylan Lewis, Alvin Poussaint, St. Clair Drake, Camille Jeffers, Robert Staples, Joyce Ladner Carrington, Robert Hill and a new breed of young Black scholars who have cast off the old white-racist oriented concept of Black families as deviant, and have come to view Black family life, in its own right, as a source and reflection of Black culture and Black consciousness.

FOUR IDEAS

Four ideas stand out in this discussion of Black families and our contribution to our struggles for survival, meaning and achievement. These are the ideas of Black culture, Black consciousness, Black community and Black competence. In each of these ideas the family is central. And the contributions the family has made to Black people and to the larger society can be described, understood and enhanced by a careful analysis of the relationship between and among these ideas and patterns of family life in the Black community.

Black Culture

In a very real sense, the question whether or not Black culture exists pales into meaninglessness when we reflect seriously on the fact and the meaning of family life among Black people. Culture refers to the totality of the ways of life of a people. It includes the basic conditions of our existence, our behavior, style of life, values, preferences and the creative expressions that emanate from our work and play. It is, in short, the way we live and have our being. There can be little doubt that the ways of life for Black folks in America is different in major respects from the ways of white folks. There are similarities, too. But the repository for the culture of a people is the family, and in the Black family resiliency, adaptability and sheer strength are primarily responsible for the fact that we as Black people have survived at all in this alien and hostile land. The heroic struggles of the Black man to hold his head high, protect his loved ones and fight off the forces who would oppress him at every turn have not been sufficiently appreciated in the writings about our people, and in the textbooks that all school children use to learn. Much of this heroism has been expressed and lived out within the intimate set of relationships which is the family.

The role of the Black woman has received more attention in considerations of the family; but even here, most of what we read about the Black woman is written by people who do not understand or care about her real triumphs and tragedies, her joys and sorrows. Yet the Black woman in America has surely withstood, endured and overcome much more oppression than any other segment of the national population. Still she remains at the bottom of the ladder of economic and political power. In the realm of the overall culture, however, she continues to reign supreme. For she continues to be the major creator, transmitter and repository of the cultural heritage of our people and the major source of socialization, guidance and inspiration for our children. All this is done best in the intimate setting of the family.

Or, consider the life and times of the Black child. There can hardly be any more severe handicaps in this country than being born poor and Black. To survive at all is a triumph. To survive with a sense of optimism, faith and commitment to life that keeps one out of trouble most of the time and enables one to contribute to the welfare of the community is even more miraculous. These are miracles performed regularly by the overwhelming majority of Black children and youth. And in the realm of creativity, whether in religion, music, art, literature, education or politics, Black youth are surely the nation's leading culture producers.

So, Black family life and Black culture are so heavily interrelated that it is hard to think of one without the other. It is well to keep this interrelationship in mind when studying about Black families, their trials and tribulations as well as their problems and their promises; their tragedies and their triumphs; their ups and their downs.

In contemporary discussions of Black culture, there are two types of culture which are often used interchangeably and sometimes without a recognition of their distinction. One type of culture refers to what might be considered the "artistic expressions of a people." This includes art, drama, literature, entertainment, music and the like. This is quite distinct from the other type of culture which refers to how a people lives. The first type of culture may be considered "entertainment culture," the second type may be considered "survival culture," for it includes the patterned ways of surviving, living and ways of doing things. This is also the type of culture described and studied by anthropologists and sociologists. The distinction between the two types is critical. Even when one or the other of these general types of culture is being considered, there are important subtypes and dimensions in each as well as important and differing conceptions.

Part of the debate about the existence of Black culture is based on differing conceptions of culture as the way of life of a people. One view of culture looks for unique and perhaps exotic artifacts; the other view looks toward the more basic patterns of behavior and values of a people. The existence and importance of Black culture does not depend, however, on its differences from other people. Its existence depends simply on its own reality; its importance depends on its functions; that is to say, its consequences for the life and death of Black people. The nature of the separate world within which Black people and white people live as well as the nature of Black culture itself must be subjected to vigorous, critical and continuous examination and discussion so that we all come to understand it better.

If our culture is unique, complex, rich and distinctive, it is, in part, because we are the sum total of our experience, and our experience as a people stems from at least four major sources. We are first and foremost an African people. Our African heritage has not been blotted out by our experience since leaving the continent. It shows in our physical features which help to condition how we behave and how we view ourselves. More importantly, our African features heavily influence how others view us and behave toward us. They are, therefore, a very important part of our contemporary culture. There are still strong among us not only physical similarities, but intellectual and common sensibilities; a sense of the importance of community, cooperation and the common good which is part of our African heritage. And beyond all that, there is that creative genius among us which expresses itself in both types of our culture. Whether in religion, music, literature, drama, dance, work and play, or in the more fundamental ways of surviving, we are coming increasingly to see that much of our African ways are still with us and have helped enable us to survive.

At the same time we are African, we are also an American people. Our culture has been shaped, in large measure, by our history and experience in America. Thus, in being American, we are also, in part, a European people. The problem for us as Americans is that while we have been forced to adopt the language and life ways of the American people in order first to serve them, and consequently to survive, we have nowhere been provided the same opportunities, privileges or resources that other Americans enjoy. Consequently, beyond being an African people, and an American people, we are an Afro-American people. Our experience in America is not like that of any other group. And most of the contributions we have made both to entertainment culture and to survival culture has grown out of this fact, and each of these major streams of civilization—African, American and Afro-American—is complex and varied within itself. Each of them is also highly interrelated in our own experience. Houston Baker has described three major aspects in which Black culture is distinctive from white American culture.

First, he observes, we are an oral and a musical people. Second, we have not succumbed to the "individualistic ethos" which is so much a part of the American character. We, as a people, are still more committed to a "collective ethos" which emphasizes the common good and common sharing. According to this view:

> Black society is not viewed as a protective arena in which the individual can work out his own destiny and gain a share of America's benefits by his own efforts. To the Black American these benefits are not attained solely by individual efforts alone, but by changes in the nature of society and the social, economic, and political advancement of a whole race of people.[1]

Finally, Baker emphasizes that because of the conditions under which we have lived in this country, much of our way of life is "repudiative." That is, we have developed the capacity and the necessity to repudiate much of what is the American way of life. And, because the American way of life is so inhuman, this critical capacity on our part is a highly valued aspect of our contribution to the nation. These three characteristics of our culture are only a beginning, for any group of Black people sitting around discussing our situation can come up with dozens of illustrations of the ways in which we are a distinct people with a distinct anchor in history, and a distinct set of life conditions. Perhaps, the Black church on Sunday morning remains one of the most widespread evidences of our ancient and contemporary sense of Black peoplehood. And, indeed, the Black family and the Black church, as they have fortified each other down through the years, have helped to keep our people alive and strong and both realistic and optimistic at the same time.

Black Consciousness

Culture, however, does not stand alone in relationship to family life. The culture does not remain alive without awareness of it and efforts to cultivate and maintain it. Thus, the idea of Black consciousness suggests that periodically in our history we become keenly aware of our common history, our common heritage and our common predicament as Black people. We become periodically aware of the contributions we can make to our own well-being and the welfare of the nation if we work together on the basis of our common interests rather than our private and individual efforts to succeed. This is one of those exciting periods in history, when in literally every walk of life and in all types of organizations and communities, we, as Black people, are saying to ourselves, our children, our friends and foes that we are somebody. We are Black and proud. We are an African people. Langston Hughes said it very well a long time ago:

> I am a Negro;
> Black as the night is black,
> Black like the depths of my Africa.

And again:

> The night is beautiful
> So the faces of my people[2]

And how many of us, particularly those over thirty, have learned the works of Langston Hughes and our other cultural heroes in our own homes and from our own families and churches? For surely, until the last few years, they did not teach them in schools. And, much more of our culture would be lost to the world if it had not been kept alive by the family.

Black Community

However conscious we might be of our culture, and however it might be enhanced by family relationships, it is clear that the family does not do it alone. The family perpetuates the culture and helps to keep it and us alive by close working relationships with the Black community. Community is a group thing. It means collective forms of life and activity. It means institutions, and it must be clear to the careful observer that the institutional fabric of the Black community is a very important source of our strength as a people. When we think of institutions in the Black community which have helped the family in carrying out its functions, none looms larger than the Black church. For it is here, in the close interaction between the family and the church, where the Black community has experienced its strongest mechanisms for survival. And if we were to single out three institutions paramount to the Black experience, they would be the family, the church and the school. Much of what Black families have achieved could not have been done without the church and the school.

It may be said that the major function of the church in our history in America has been to enable us to endure the conditions of our existence, and to turn some of our adversities into constructive programs for our advancement. Though the influence of the organized church is waning among us, it is still hard to find an adult of any substance who does not owe his or her accomplishments to the spiritual resources of our people, as often reflected jointly in the family and the church. Historically, the church has helped to confirm the sense that we are somebody. We are God's children. It has also provided opportunities for expression, leadership and organization that were denied us elsewhere. Many of the leading Black educators, professionals, entertainers, government officials, as well as most plain hard-working folk, got their start or were helped along the way by the combined forces of church and family. There are other institutions and persons in the Black community who have often come to the aid of the family in meeting its responsibilities. The sense of community responsibility is still a major aspect of our communities; though it is dying too and needs to be recaptured, it is still alive in churches, schools, clubs, athletics, peer groups, informal associations and various neighborhood crossroads where people meet each other in ordinary activities.

Black Competence

One of the major goals and achievements among our Black families is developing a sense of competence on the part of individual family members, especially the young. Families must instill in the young a sense of mastery, a quest for achievement, a set of interpersonal skills and the desire to acquire technical skills in order to function in the world. The fact that most Black children do, in fact, acquire these basic competencies within the framework of their families is a tribute to the effectiveness of Black family life. The fact that many do not achieve these qualities is a measure of the odds against which the families must struggle. The goal of Black family life, then, is to produce competent individuals, people able to be, to know, to do and above all, to think. These are the requisites of survival.

So we see that it is difficult to think of our families in isolation, and do us justice, or understand us properly, or enhance our functioning. We are intimately involved in a culture and community. Our mission is not simply to exist and certainly not simply to conform to what other families look like or do, but to produce competent individuals able to conquer some major aspects of our inner and outer environments in order to survive, perpetuate the race and make some contributions to the larger society. Let us consider some brief references to Black people as illustrations.

These vignettes from the lives of ordinary Black people are designed to help illustrate the interrelatedness of Black culture and forces in the Black community which help to produce and sustain a high level of competence among Black people. They are the kind of examples that any one of us might recall from our own experience and observations living in the Black community. They are the kind of people who might very well live next door to us. They are selected here because sketches from their lives have been made available in the public press or some other public media. Names of persons and places have been changed.

- Let us consider first the story of Mrs. Mary Thomas. In typical sociological fashion, she could be described in very negative terms. She could be described as a mother of ten children who has no husband. In addition, several of her children are school dropouts; at least one has gotten in trouble and one is currently institutionalized. Living in the heart of a metropolitan area on the east coast she might very well be characterized as an example of a problem family in the Black community. But people who know her and her situation have a very different image altogether.

Like so many of us, Mrs. Thomas was born in the South. In her case, she was born in a small southern town where she went to high school, and for a year attended the local state college, but was not able to continue. She moved north in 1945, was married and divorced and worked as a clerk in a store in order to support her family.

She is a Christian woman and much of the source of her own remarkable achievement, which we will mention below, may be attributed to her deep sense of spiritual commitment and her strong striving for education for herself and her children. She has been very active in her church and a past vice-president of a women's Christian service association. She is a Sunday-school teacher, a class leader in the youth department and has also worked with the church choir. In addition, she has also done volunteer work in other community organizations.

Perhaps a most remarkable feature of Mrs. Thomas' accomplishment is that in June of 1971 she graduated from college after many years' delay and long hard work. At the same time, she shared these graduation honors with three of her children. She managed to complete a college education while raising her family, working part-time and participating in at least a dozen church, school, civic and youth organizations.

• Mr. and Mrs. Roosevelt T. Smith also live in an urban community in the North with their two daughters and one son. At age 35, Mrs. Smith has returned to school studying at the local community college in order to pursue her advanced studies toward a bachelor's degree after 18 years of being out of high school. She graduated from high school in 1953 but was unable to go on to college. She took a government job, as so many young Black high-school graduates aspired to do in those years. In 1969, however, she began part-time study. She has recently become a recipient of a scholarship which will enable her to study full-time. In addition to being a wife and mother, she is active in community affairs and is a leader in the Future Business Leaders of America.

• When Mrs. Harriet B. Wilson was a high-school student in Alabama and took a course in printing, little did she know that her own skills at printing and communications would lead her to the top of the publishing program of her national church organization.

With her husband, Rev. Wilson, she has given tremendous leadership in her church organization at the local level for several years. Together they edited the handbook for the missionary department of their church district.

She finished her college work at a small Black college in Alabama and completed a master's degree in library science at a white school in Tennessee where she was among the top six students in her graduating class. She has been a public school librarian and has served as President of the PTA and as Director of the Christian Education Department of her church district. Mrs. Wilson, whose husband is now deceased, is the mother of four children and has five grandchildren. All of her children are successfully established.

• It is said that when Mrs. Wilhemena Barnes was growing up along the Gulf Coast of Mississippi during the early 1900's, her childhood dream was to have "a huge house which would gather in all the unwanted children." She has been quoted in a national newspaper as saying, "I knew all the heartaches and disappointments. I know what it is like to be unwanted, unloved and rejected." Now at age 70, having been married for fifty-one years to the Rev. James Barnes, a Methodist minister in a small Mississippi town, Mrs. Barnes has had a long career of realizing her childhood dream. Together with her husband, family and friends, she has helped to rear more than forty children who were abandoned or neglected along with rearing five of her own children.

At age 19 she married Rev. Barnes and their five children were all born in Mississippi in the depths of the Depression. In addition to their own five children, they took in a five-month old baby whose mother was dying. This was the beginning of their career as foster parents. That baby is now a 37-year-old jazz musician and bandleader of some note. He has accomplished this despite the fact that during his boyhood he was labeled by authorities as mentally retarded. The Barnes family knew and loved him as a very precious child and they nurtured his tremendous talent. Mrs. Barnes gave part of the answer for the tremendous success they have had with children who are considered by others to be mentally retarded. "The most they need is love and understanding. They're starved for love, and if you show them any affection you can get them to do almost anything."

She recently received national honors and was awarded a $5,000 prize for her outstanding volunteer service. On that occasion she was quoted as saying, "I never before in my life knew so much money all at once." Presently, Rev. and Mrs. Barnes live in a nine-room house in a little southern country town where they care for eleven children, two of whom they have adopted. Mrs. Barnes was abandoned by both her parents by the time she was 5 years old, and she and her younger brother were cared for by relatives in Mississippi, Alabama and Louisiana. She said, "We never stayed in one place long. I'd gone to five elementary schools before I finished sixth grade." Despite the hardship, Mrs. Barnes was obviously provided with a very loving and effective upbringing.

Mrs. Barnes was only able to complete nine grades of education during her formative years. Recently, however, she has completed night school courses and earned a high school equivalency diploma. She is currently taking college courses in an effort to get a degree in special education so that, "I can try to help the children more."

• When Mrs. Saralee Weatherford was honored by the military as Wife of the Year, the press reported her as stating that the military had given her husband and her opportunities that they never would have known in their midwestern hometown. She was chosen from among more than one thousand candidates nominated by military wives' organizations throughout the world, and she was the first Black woman to attain this title. She has been married for eighteen years to Mr. Weatherford who is one of the highest ranking Black officers in the United States Army. They have five children and although the children are away at school, Mrs. Weatherford has been very active in community activities in overseas locations, including the PTA, Girl Scouts, Catholic church activities and in European-American intercultural activities. When someone reflected on the fact that she grew up in poverty as did her husband, she was quick to indicate that life was not all bleak: "Yes, it was a very sad situation, but it was happy too. I had a lot of love, a lot of care." She is an only child, brought up by her mother who saw her through college and Mr. Weatherford is one of seven children. Mrs. Weatherford has described part of their philosophy: "We didn't have a lot of hangups when we were growing up. We knew there was a better life out there somewhere so we went after it." She has a rather positive conception of the opportunities the military has provided for her husband: "The Army gave my husband the opportunity to do something dignified. It's made a good life for us, we love it." When asked about the problems other men seem to have in the service, she pointed out a very important distinction: "But you must understand, that we live as a family unit—my husband and I and the children. That's a lot different from men living together in the barracks. Their experiences may be completely different."

• In *Guideposts Magazine*,[3] there is an article on a young Black basketball player's rise to fame. I will call him Jesse Foster. In many respects Jesse was and is an ordinary Black American youth. As a kid growing up in new England, young Jesse dreamed of being a professional basketball player. His problem, however, was that he was short. As a sophomore in high school he was still only 5'8" and he had often been told that he could never be successful in basketball. But Jesse had a love for the sport ever since he was a lad in school. He felt that if he were going to achieve anything in life besides being just another Black kid hanging around the block that it would come from basketball. He was the smallest of six children in his family, but figured that he would someday sprout up because his mother, who had once played with a touring women's basketball team was six feet.

Jesse's family had a modest income and he felt that by excelling in basketball he might win a scholarship to college. During the summer before he entered the tenth grade, Jesse went to see his family minister, Reverend Louis Jefferson, pastor of the A. M. E. Church. He had counseled with Rev. Jefferson many times during his young life, sometimes about problems he had with other kids or with the authorities when he broke some windows and sometimes about his homework. However, when he talked with the pastor on this occasion, he was feeling very sorry for himself; he had decided that he was too small to do anything, much less play basketball. Rev. Jefferson talked to him about God and about prayer. He told Jesse not to pray to gain inches, but for help in making the best of his height and talent.

Jesse later became an outstanding high school and college athlete. During his senior year in college, he was picked in the professional draft. Again he was successful. In the article he relates that he became a regular on the team and was accepted by the other professionals. Giants like Kareem Abdul-Jabbar and Wilt Chamberlain found they couldn't ignore him on the court. Jesse won the respect of his teammates who began looking to him for scoring the clutch points.

Jesse remembers much of his childhood. Many of his boyhood dreams had already come true, but he found himself with a strong desire to go back to his hometown and work with underprivileged Black kids. He feels a special relationship to youngsters who feel they can't succeed because he was once in their shoes before he learned to stop wishing for something he didn't have and concentrate on making the most of what he did have. Jesse, who is now a star player with a top pro team, is still one of the smallest players in the national association. He is another outstanding example of Black competence.

Each of these sketches tells something about the life of ordinary people. These are the kind of people who very well may be next-door neighbors. In fact, any one of us might multiply this list a hundred times over from people who live next door, around the corner, down the street or up the road; from people who attend the same church, school or belong to the same club or association. In fact, a striking fact about life in the Black community is that most of the people we know are ordinary people who do not conform to the statistical reports of us that other people write. However, these sketches also show, and a careful reflection of our own experiences in the Black community will support, that the road to competence and achievement is a precarious one for all of us. The sources, proofs and measures of the success of Black Americans are many and varied.

In my book, *Black Families in White America*,[4] I describe this process as screens of opportunity. These screens come at various levels of our social organization. Sometimes they are evident in the individual talent or ability of very young children and youth as they grow older. It is necessary to be conscious of this when one associates with people and observes others. Often, however, this innate ability and talent is not harnessed. What is necessary is to have this ability nurtured in the intimate relation of family and loved ones. Thus, the family plays a critical role in helping to instill in young people a sense of somebodyness, a sense of aspiration and the courage to strive hard to attain meaningful goals. Outside the family, in the Black community, there is another level of social reality that often provides screens of opportunity for our young people that is generally not taken into consideration in sociological studies. In this respect, the church, school and Black community play an inordinately strong role. Sometimes the opportunities provided for young people to achieve comes from an individual, sometimes the minister, sometimes a choir director, sometimes a Sunday-school teacher, sometimes a school teacher, a principal, a band leader, a boy scout leader, football coach, sometimes the ordinary folks next door. Beyond the level of the Black community, however, lies the wider white society which sometimes provides opportunities for some of our youth while it systematically denies the same to others. It is by taking strategic advantage of these opportunities that our families and our communities have enabled our young people to reach high levels of achievement and competence. I think from reflecting on such processes of achievement that we learn the importance of taking advantage of the opportunities provided at each of these levels of society to enhance the well-being and sense of competence of Black youth and adults as well. And again, we see the importance of a conscious recognition of our culture as a people and a conscious development of the strengths of our communities, as important instruments for the movement of our people into the larger areas of society on the basis of competence and mastering of that society and not on the basis of weakness and dependency.

There are some Black families in America headed by men and women who have reached extraordinary levels of achievement. Sometimes it is said that these people pulled themselves up by their own bootstraps. Sometimes it is said that they are exceptional people and are a credit to their race. Sometimes it is said that they represent stronger and more stable family lives than the rest of us. All these are very simplistic explanations that grow more out of ignorance than out of a realistic understanding of the complexities of Black family and community life. In my view the major distinction between extraordinary Black people and ordinary Black people is that the extraordinary ones have been provided with a greater measure of opportunities. They are not any brighter, or more able, moral, virtuous or hard working than the rest of us. They have been blessed by the screens of opportunities in ways denied the majority of Black people, and this accounts for their remarkable achievements. It is sometimes said, also, that Black families of high levels of achievement have escaped the disadvantage of the association of being Black in American society. This is also a misguided conception, for being Black is still by far the most important characteristic of our existence. It is far more important than any of the other virtues associated with success and achievement. And Black people of extraordinary achievement are still subjected to indignities and discriminations and are denied opportunities often available to ordinary white people.

These families represent sources of achievement at each of the societal levels—the individual, the family, the Black community and the larger society which have helped to make and sustain them in their present positions. It is increasingly clear to me that achieving families in the Black community are more and more aware of both the sources and the precariousness of their achievement. Five women who represent some of these achieving families spoke with a reporter of a national newspaper and the story was published in 1968. They are suggestive of the point I am making. The average woman in the story was in her mid-forties. Two of them were born in the North and three in the South. All of them hold bachelor degrees and three of them hold advanced degrees. Four of them are married and one is divorced. Of those married, three have children ranging in ages from 8 to 24 years. Two of these families live in a suburb of New York, two live in an upper-middle class section of Harlem and one family has residences both in New York City and New Jersey. All of the men in these families are professionals. Among them are an electronics engineer, a physician, a research scientist and a judge. All of their children of age have gone or are about to go to college. They represent high levels of achievement in Black families in America.

These women represent the fact that the working wife and mother is a strong feature of the success of many Black families. One of these women, for example, is a former reporter and editor for a large

Black newspaper and was a high-level civil servant in her state. Another was principal of a secondary school and was a district school superintendent. A third was a registered nurse who was active in community work. Another was formerly an executive director of an important model neighborhood antipoverty agency. A fifth woman was formerly co-director of a community development unit in another antipoverty program agency.

One of the women talked about the struggle to achieve and to help the family meet its responsibilities at the same time. At the height of activity, when her children were young and there was the commuting and the job and the husband who was not quite established in his career, and there was the whole syndrome of entertaining, belonging to women's clubs and serving on boards, her life seemed more organized than it had been before or since. It is not an unusual occurrence for so-called middle-class wives and mothers to work. This mother says that if a woman is attending to all her basic needs and responsibilities—as wife, mother and a person who needs an outlet for expression in the world outside the home, whether as a paid professional or volunteer—there is more energy available for each one of them and all things go better. The difficulty arises when a woman is ambivalent about her roles and is not free to relate to them in a balanced way.

It often happens, however, that in making opportunities for competent and successful Black women, the larger society often uses Black women to help discriminate against Black men. One of the women interviewed was very sensitive to that problem. As an executive in a large and important white firm, she often senses that Black men in the company resent her for the position in which they are cast. She often wishes she were not there because she feels it's doing something to destroy a little bit of them to see her in an executive position. She said she would never compete directly with a Black man for a particular job because the larger society needs to have aggressive Black males competing for those titles and salaries and positions and that most Black women would never stand in the way of this kind of progress.

Life is not rosy and is far from equal even for Black women and mothers in the higher levels of the achieving society. One of these mothers expressed the view that the Black woman has to deal with the prejudice and discrimination she experiences too—in the market place, in the schools with the children, in committees on which she may serve, or her own job. She has to handle not only her own resentments of the day, but understand those of her husband and children. She said that the Black woman has to somehow give the kind of support that will enable everyone to go out the next morning and deal with "The Problem" over and over again. During the last few years since these particular women were talking about their situation, the momentum to achieve has increased and Black women are even more expressive of their situation today.

Part of the realization of privileged Black families of the commonality and sense of community of all Black families is expressed by a number of Black people who had deserted the Black community, but returned to it in spirit and activity. In a newspaper article a couple of years ago, a young Black writer described the return of a number of middle-class Black families to active identification with the struggle of Black people in Harlem. His particular report is only suggestive of a much larger trend. He tells, for example, of a young, articulate market analyst who moved to Harlem with his wife and children. The young man was somewhat apprehensive as he walked with his briefcase to his job in the white community and was greeted by two middle-aged Black men sitting on a stoop who seemed to be recuperating from a hangover. They raised their heads and said to him pleasantly, "Good morning." His apprehension subsided when he discovered that they were sincere and nothing but friendly to his wife and children. Later, he struck up an association with them which eventually aided them in their own economic development. He also discovered that the Black shopkeepers in the neighborhood were friendly; he became a regular customer of theirs and began to feel that their respect was firm enough to bear his offering them some advice about store management. He suggested to one grocer that his business would improve if he removed the cluttered and dirty flypaper dangling from the ceiling, rearranged the stock on his shelves, tidied up the shop a bit and kept better books. The grocer was grateful, and followed the young man's advice with appreciation and to his advantage.

To another grocer whose meats were particularly good, the young analyst suggested he convert his store to a butcher shop and become the neighborhood butcher to better compete in business. The grocer took this advice and was also successful. This young analyst has made himself a very popular and respected member of the community and has become the informal management consultant to nearly all the neighborhood shopkeepers, advising them on such matters as bookkeeping, advertising and buying. He does this in addition to his major occupation "downtown."

One young Black lawyer in the neighborhood conducts reading classes for kids after school. He was quoted as saying, "I am forced to return their total honesty and be constant in my attention to them." Another Black professional, an engineer who lives in what he considers a particularly rough block, described his neighbors as follows: "The teenage boys who have reputations for trouble, breaking into stores and that sort of thing and all the people too, let me walk around the neighborhood without harm because I'm sensitive about what I say to them and talk to them as a regular fellow and they think I'm a nice, square guy." An accountant has given a great deal of free advice to shopkeepers about keeping their books or visits with them and talks politics. He was quoted, "I've heard from the shopkeepers I help or talk politics with, that at least seven young girls say I am their ideal fellow."

The point is simply this, when men and women of achievement seek to identify with their culture and their community, they are welcomed by ordinary people. This process has been going on at an increased pace during the past few years in all parts of the country. It is indeed one of the indications that despite the so-called social class barrier, Black families, within the context of the Black community, have a great deal of promise for unity and for pulling together for the common good of the Black community. Unfortunately, many of us do not take proper advantage of this opportunity and its potential for unity. We are still victimized by the misconceptions of us generated by other people, and we allow these so-called divisions to separate us unnecessarily.

THE ROLE OF WOMEN IN THE FAMILY AND IN THE COMMUNITY

Any discussion of Black families and the struggle for survival must give special attention to the role of women, as the illustrations above help to make clear. Any contemporary discussion of the role of Black women must take special note of the imbalance in the male-female ratio in the Black community. In her recent studies, Professor Jacquelyne J. Jackson of Duke University, has pointed out that there are considerably more Black females than Black males and that situation has become more critical since 1850, more than a hundred years ago. In several states and many communities the number of young Black women is much greater than the number of young Black men. In addition to the absolute ratio, when we consider the fact that Black men are much more likely to be drafted into the armed services and much more likely to be incarcerated in prisons and jails than any other group in the population, we can begin to appreciate the relative shortage of Black men, particularly between the ages of 18 to 35. According to Dr. Jackson this relative unavailability of Black men may account more for the presence of female-headed families in the Black community than all of the sociological explanations offered by other scholars.

According to the 1970 U.S. Census,[5] females constituted 53 percent of the population of the Black community. This was an increase over the 52 percent in 1960 and the 51 percent in 1950. There were nearly twelve million Black females in 1970. Thus, whether we speak of potential voters, college students, those in need of day-care services or those who are unemployed, Black females constituted the majority of the Black population in the U.S. and has nearly doubled in the thirty years between 1940 and 1970. One reason for the increase of females over males in the Black community is that females live longer than males. Black women have a life expectancy considerably shorter than that of American women as a whole, but significantly longer than that of Black men.

One of the areas which is grossly misunderstood by the general reading public is the contribution Black women make to family stability and achievement. When one considers the hazards of growing up Black and poor and female in a society which is largely hostile to these groups, and the toll which these pressures exact, it is of considerable significance to note that most Black women who have ever been married were still married and living with their husbands at the time of the 1970 Census. We know historically that this has been true since the end of the Civil War. And for each year since 1950, the proportion of Black families who meet this particular criterion for stability ranges between 81 percent and 96 percent, although it is true that there has been a 5 percent decrease in marital stability since 1950. This is hardly a remarkable shift, however, considering the tremendous social changes which have occurred in the last twenty years in most aspects of American life and considering the unavailability of young Black males.

The concept of female-heads of families has received a great deal of attention in the literature and while it is true that nearly one-third of Black families may be so described, it is not always clear who these women are and what contributions they make to their family and community. The overwhelming majority of these women have been married. Only about 16 percent are single. Nearly one-half of them are separated or divorced from their husbands and nearly a third have maintained their families after their husbands died. It is of even more significance to note that 53 percent of these mothers (slightly more than half) and their families live in poverty, subsisting on less than $3000 a year despite the fact that the overwhelming majority of them work for a living and are self-supporting. It is of equal importance to note, however, that nearly half of these women, or about 47 percent function above the poverty level. How is it possible to escape the more debilitating aspects of poverty, if you are Black, and female, and have three children, and no husband? We are fully aware, as Dr. Robert Hill has recently pointed out in his book, *Strengths of Black Families,*[6] that the wages paid to Black women are lower than those paid to any other category of American workers. The fact then, that nearly half of the Black women who are heads of families manage to keep themselves and their children operating above the poverty level is a minor miracle which deserves not only celebration, but thorough examination. It may well be that we could gain considerable new insight into the contributions these women make to our society and into the tribute their society exacts from them. For it is one thing to stay out of poverty when the institutions of the dominant society work for you. It is quite another thing when they ignore you or conspire against you. An understanding of how Black women accomplish this feat would record not only their strengths, but the places in the structure of the larger society amenable and responsive to their strengths.

It has become increasingly clear over the past few years that Black women make an important contribution to the economic as well as the social stability of family life. Again, however, this role has been subjected to great misinterpretations. It is true, that a substantial proportion, roughly 44 percent of Black women with children under five years of age participate actively in the labor force. It is not true, however, as some reports suggest, that Black women are the major breadwinners in their communities. Thus, among husband and wife families, a third of the women who work contribute less than a fifth of the total family income and only 13 percent contribute as much as half of the total family income. Among the poorest of Black families where it is generally held that women are the primary breadwinners, their total contribution to the family income is even less. Thus, among families with incomes of $3000 and under, in 1970 nearly a half of the women who worked contributed less than twenty cents of every dollar of family income. What this means is that despite the fact that the vast majority of Black women work, their wages and job security are so low and unemployment among them is so high that their contribution to total family income is considerably less than their efforts and commitment would demand. One of the major reasons for the depressed level of earnings by Black women is the occupational discrimination to which they are subjected. Black women who are heads of families and have to work are subjected to more occupational discrimination than other women. Thus, roughly 16 percent of Black married women are in the highest occupational category of professional workers. This is true of 13 percent of single and nearly 8 percent of those who are separated and divorced. When we consider all of these so-called middle-class occupations combined, we observe that nearly 65 percent of the single women who work occupy these white collar and skilled occupations. This is true of 55 percent of the married women who work, but only 43 percent of those who are separated from their husbands. What this means is that in the lower ranks of service workers and domestics is where the majority of these mothers earn their livelihood to support their families. The earnings of Black women vary considerably not only by occupation, but by the age and education of workers. Thus, the median income of Black women in 1969 was $4126. This is only 80 percent as much as the median income for white women. Black women between the ages of 35 and 44 seem to have the most favorable earnings. Their median income was $4556 which means that half of them earned more than this amount and half earned less and this median income was 86 percent of the median income for white women in the same age range.

It helps considerably if you are a working Black woman to have finished high school and college. Whatever the level of educational attainment, however, it does not equalize the earning of Black women with white women, even on the same jobs, but it does improve the earning of Black women relative to their less educated sisters. Thus, Black women who had completed eighth grade had a median income of $1320 in 1969. Their sisters with high school educations had a median income of $3257 and those who had completed college had a median income of $6747.

It is not generally appreciated that a fundamental distinction exists between why Black people live in poverty and why white people live in poverty. Essentially, white people who are poor are poor because they don't work. This is not the case with Black people. Blacks are more likely to be poor despite the fact that they work. Thus in 1969, among Black families headed by males, 18 percent had a total family income below $3000. In the majority of these families the husband and father had a job and in half of these families he worked full time, every day, all year round. Still his earnings and those of his wife were not sufficient to pull these families out of poverty. In the case of white families headed by men, only 6 percent had incomes below $3000 in 1970 and only about a third of them worked full time.

The situation is even more striking when we observe the work and poverty status of female-headed families. Thus, in 1970, 53 percent of families headed by females had total incomes below the poverty level despite the fact that four-fifths of these women worked and half of them worked full time the whole year. Among white female-headed families who were poor, less than one-sixth of them worked full time.

We know, of course, that some of the major reasons people don't work is that they cannot find a job or they are sick and incapacitated. We know also, however, that these problems are much more prevalent among Black people, yet since not working is such an important cause of poverty among white people, it may well be that the only major group of poor white people left are the aged, the halt, the lame and the blind. For the society is so structured that the opportunities for economic viability do in fact exist for ordinary white people. The fact, however, that so many Black people are poor despite the fact that they work hard everyday all year round, and despite the fact that often two or three members of the family work is a further commentary on the structure of a society whose economic viability is largely built on the suffering of poor Black people. The call us lazy, but surely we are now and historically among the hardest working people in the world. Yet the rewards are not nearly commensurate with our efforts or the rewards received by others, or the capacity of the society to sustain its citizens. This situation places a tremendous strain on the viability of the family. The fact that the Black family functions as well as it does against these odds is a tribute to its resilience, its strengths and its adaptability. And in all these respects the Black woman plays an important, if grossly misunderstood role.

SUGGESTED QUESTIONS FOR STUDY GROUPS

1. What is meant by "entertainment culture"? "Survival culture"?
2. Do you agree that much of the Black man's way of life is "repudiative?" If no, why? If yes, illustrate some of the ways in which this "critical capacity" expresses itself.
3. How do you respond to Billingsley's statement: "Though the influence of the organized church is waning among us, it is still hard to find an adult of any substance who does not owe his accomplishments to the spiritual resources of our people often reflected jointly in his family and his church?" (cf. study text page 18).
4. What is mean by "screens of opportunity?" Illustrate. In what ways might the church assist persons in taking greater advantage of the "screens of opportunity?"
5. Identify some of the ways in which the larger society uses Black women to discriminate against Black men.
6. How do you respond to Billingsley's statement: ". . . when men

and women of achievement seek to identify with their culture and their community, they are welcomed by ordinary people?" (cf. study text page 29).
7. Illustrate ways in which the conceptions of others about us have served to create divisions among us.
8. In what ways do Black women experience occupational discrimtion? Illustrate.

2

we are an african people

We are an African people. That is what students on the Howard University radio station WHUR in Washington, D.C., call "A Black fact." It is a fact we in the Black community are not yet fully aware of and appreciate. And yet, the fact of our Africaness is something of which we must become increasingly aware and must teach to our children. For this is one way of dealing with the important question of our sense of somebodyness. It is a necessary approach to dealing with the question of who we are as a people; where do we come from and where are we going? To say that we are an African people is to raise the important question, what do we mean by Africa? In a sense there are two Africas for us. First, there is the Africa of our heritage. By this I mean ancient Africa which is the cradle of human civilization itself. I refer to that portion of the world where our ancestors lived in relative peace and harmony before being discovered and exploited first by the Arabs and later by the Europeans.

That is the Africa of our heritage which is that portion of West Africa in which our ancestors were captured and sold into slavery.

There is at the same time, however, a second Africa which is no less indispensable to our sense of being as a people: The modern contemporary Africa. We are also a part of that, and when I say the Black community more and more I speak of the existence of people of African heritage wherever they are anywhere in the world. We must teach ourselves and our children about this Africa as well as about the ancient Africa of our heritage.

In a recent meeting at Harvard University a Black professor was being very critical of the curriculum in the Afro-American Studies Department. When the students described, with a great deal of excitement, a course being taught on East African development, he said, "But Black people in America didn't come from East Africa." He was expressing a very typical misconception about what Africa is to Black people. He would confine our Africa to the West Coast of Africa from which the slaves were captured. There are a number of reasons why we must continue to reassert and appreciate our Africaness, but among the most compelling is that by identifying ourselves as African, we emphasize the fact that we are not a small insignificant minority on the world scene. Some people say to us, "You are only a minority group. You represent only 10 percent of the nation's population, therefore you should not expect all the rights and privileges enjoyed by the majority." Sometimes they even try to convince us that it is democratic that we should accept something less than full human rights. It is even true that some of our own leaders refer to us as a minority and use that 10 percent figure to help emphasize our powerlessness and our sense of nobodyness. It is strange that we should find so acceptable this conception of ourselves as a minority. In the very same country nobody ever tells the Jewish people, "You are only 3 percent of the nation's population, therefore you do not deserve to have preeminence in the fields of finance, communication, entertainment and education," where they enjoy a sense of presence, power, influence and rewards way out of proportion to their numbers. They did not reach this sense of preeminence by telling themselves that they are only an insignificant minority. They did it by identifying themselves positively and insisting on capitalizing on their particular assets and the particular weaknesses and vulnerabilities of others. It is not unusual to find communities where most of the citizens are Black, but most of the teachers and school administrators are Jewish and most of the merchants are Jewish, and where the lawyers, social science professionals and government officials are also part of that community. Nor is it surprising to find a strong sense of solidarity and cooperation among this ethnic group. It is very similar in other ethnic groups as well. When we say we are an African people we are not being anti-semitic or anti-white, but we are endeavoring to find the sources of our own strength to build our own communities and our own competence and to strengthen our capacity for contributing to our own governance and our own welfare.

When we say then, that we are an African people, we are increasingly aware that there are a variety of Africas. St. Clair Drake has written a new book which traces the existence of a culture of African people in all parts of the world. He shows the important cultural values which connect us, including the very important spiritual quality which may be found in a variety of forms wherever African people live. In a chapter of his book called "The Redemption of Africa and Black Religion," published in 1972 as a separate pamphlet by the Third World Press, Drake points out that, as an African people, we are also a religious people. In the introduction to this pamphlet, Vincent Harding refers to it as follows:

> ... we are really presented with three important, related thematic lines. The first sketches an overview of the development of African cultures in the New World. ... Drake goes on to deal with experience of black religion in North America and the Carribean, indicating the crucial role of religion in our struggles towards freedom, identity and self-determination. Finally, ... Drake deals with the development of a mode of thinking which he calls "Ethiopianism" and the concept of "Providential Design" as developed in the centuries of our exile and returns.[1]

As African people, then, the Black community exists in every major part of the world and as I have pointed out elsewhere, with the exception of Greenland, Black people have important presence on each of the important land masses of the world. There are, then, seven major concentrations of African peoples. The first and most important concentration is on the African continental mainland itself. In 1972 there were between 4 and 5 hundred million Africans on the mainland and with a population increase of 2.8 percent each year, it is clear that by the year 2000 when many of us will still be alive and our children will be adults, there will be between 7 and 9 hundred million brothers and sisters on the mainland. Already Africa constitutes the largest population group outside modern China.

The second largest concentration of Africans in the modern world is in the United States. There are more than 30 million Black people living in this country alone. Three facts are increasingly clear to us about the Black presence in America. First, the economic development of the country would not have been possible were it not for the participation of the Black people. Second, there would be no original American contribution to world culture in music, art, literature, dance, athletics and increasingly in social science were it not for the Black presence in America. And third, it is increasingly clear to us that if the nation is ever to reassert the most basic sense of humanity ascribed by peace, love, fellowship and community, it will be because the nation pays attention to the Black presence in its midst. It is hard, when thinking of these facts, to think of ourselves as an insignificant minority.

The third largest concentration of Africans is in South America. There are between 25 and 28 million Africans in that part of the world. It is perhaps from South America more than any other place in the New World where Africans have made a strong impact on the culture of that region. This is due, in part, to the fact that Africans outnumbered Europeans in such large numbers in the early years of the settlement of that important continent.

The fourth largest concentration of Africans is in the West Indies. The rise of "Black Power" in the Indies in recent years is a striking indication of the potency of the Black presence in that region. The interrelatedness between Africans on the U.S. mainland and Africans in the West Indies is strikingly illustrated by the manner in which the Black colleges of the South have provided a strong resource of education for West Indians at a time when they were not allowed to matriculate to other universities in this country. This is exemplified by the fact that the largest concentration of West Indian students in this country is at Howard University in Washington, D.C. At commencement in 1972, two Governors of independent West Indian countries, both graduates of Howard University, were given honorary degrees. This awareness of the Africaness of West Indians and U.S. Blacks is being expressed on that campus by students and faculty alike as they evolve into new patterns of collaboration and interaction.

The fifth largest concentration of Africans is in Europe, where in 1972 there were between 5 and 7 million Africans. It is not without note that much of the movement toward African unity has been organized in Europe. In modern times this was exemplified by the fact that in 1944 George Padmore, Peter Milliard and T. Ras Makonnen together with Kwame Nkrumah merged their efforts in the establishment of the Pan-African Federation in Manchester, England. They were responsible for the holding of the Fifth Pan-African Congress in Manchester in 1945. It may also be noted that the First and Second International Conferences of Black Writers, sponsored by the Society for African Culture, were held in Paris in 1956 and Rome in 1959. Not all Black people in Europe are intellectuals—not even a majority. In fact, St. Clair Drake's own doctoral dissertation was done by studying the Black community of merchant seamen and workers who lived in Wales. The various wars fought by European powers which involved Black people in their overseas territories have been a major source of the migration of Africans to Europe. In addition, some opportunities provided in Europe for economic and educational pursuit have also attracted many Africans to that continent. Their presence has often been a troubling matter for the Europeans, particularly as they have sought to advance themselves economically. Their presence and contribution to European culture has not been sufficiently appreciated.

The sixth largest concentration of Africans is in Mexico and Central America where between 2 and 3 million Africans are presently residing. In some respects, Africans have been more readily absorbed into the European culture of those civilizations than in other parts of the world.

Finally, a seventh major concentration of Africans is in Canada and Nova Scotia where between 1 and 2 million Africans reside today.

Thus, when we think of ourselves as African people spread out in major concentrations and smaller ones all over the world, including a major concentration of Black people in Russia and China, we can see that we are not a small, insignificant minority. We are an important part of the world's people and as we come more and more to sense ourselves as a community we'll be more and more able to exert an impact and a healing influence on world civilization. To the extent that we are able to appreciate this and teach this to our children, we will be able to enhance the development of our own sense of peoplehood and somebodyness. This is an important part of what Africa means to us and what it means to be and to say that we are an African people.

AFRICAN HERITAGE

When we think about our African heritage, we are increasingly aware that we are not an African people because of our pigmentation, the texture of our hair and other physical features; but we are African in a deeper sense because those characteristics are somewhat transitory. Being African also means having a sense of reality. It means having a sense of the orderliness of nature. It means having a sense of rhythm. It means having a sense that there is rhythm not only in us, but there is rhythm in nature too, and that we should be tuned in to the universe. Rhythm is tied in to a whole philosophy of life.

We are an African people and some characteristics of Africa have remained with us because they are deeper than some of the more superficial aspects of culture. People who look at us and say, "Well, there's no African culture left," look for simple artifacts such as if our food is the same as that of Africans four hundred years ago. Do we still speak the same languages? They conclude that we must be Americans because we're speaking the American language, and so on. But the search for our Africaness must go much deeper than that. We must look for a way of looking at the world, a way of relating to the world, our way of sensing who we are, and our way of struggling to survive and helping others to survive. Those are some of the characteristics that we have brought with us from Africa.

There is a great deal of misconception in literature about what

African family life was like before the coming of the Europeans. Not only is there the notion of savagery, but there are also basic misconceptions of various patterns of family life. The pattern of dominance—male/female dominance—is fallaciously related in literature today. The pattern of family forms, the whole matter of polygyny in which a man has two or more wives at the same time, and polygamy in which a man or a woman has two or more spouses at the same time, is very misleading in literature. I doubt that few except the most careful students of Black history have gone into these matters, and yet, they are very important to African life and they should be clarified. The need for clarification is necessary for understanding ourselves and for interpreting our African past to our children as well as to the rest of the world. We need an historical perspective in order to understand the nature of family life and in order to see the connections between family life in Africa and family life in the Americas and even in the United States, for there are distinct continuities that exist.

Not only do we need to understand the nature of African family life in Africa before the coming of the white man, we also need to understand what happened on the arrival of the white man. We need to understand the impact of the slave trade, and we need to understand not only the reasons for it, but also the consequences of it. Historical analysis, then, must teach us, help us to understand and reanalyze the nature of the slave trade and its particular impact on family life. The economics of the slave trade led to the gathering up of young men, particularly men 14 years old and over, or sometimes younger than that. There was a tremendous emphasis on young men because they were considered physically stronger and more profitable and not quite as difficult to handle as women. For centuries that had a tremendous impact on the balance between men and women in the Black community. And it had tremendous impact on many of the practices that developed because of that imbalance. On many plantations there was something like nine men to every woman and that had tremendous consequences for the evolution of forming the family life.

It is very commonly said that slavery in America was so rigid, so inhuman and so effective that it cut off all of our African sensibilities and converted us into a new kind of human being—an American, a

Negro. That view of Black people in the Americas is so common it's hard to find a contrary view in history. Pick up any treatment on Black families, and with few exceptions, you'll find the statement over and over again in a variety of ways, that slavery obliterated all traces of Africa. Now, of course, this history was written first by white people and some Black people have copied it because, as you know, we tend to absorb the views of ourselves that are put forth by the majority that are current, particularly those that are considered authoritative. So, we have been echoing that view to Africa—that slavery cut off everything. Let's just analyze that idea and the reasons that it received such strong support in face of the impossibility of its being true.

Take any people who have spent centuries developing a certain culture, a certain way of life anywhere in the world, and subject them to the most cruel punishment, like the concentration camps, and continue that for a hundred years. Still it is not possible to obliterate all traces of their history. A people become human because of their heritage and their history and you cannot obliterate *all* of that; it's impossible. Slavery did not change some things that are obvious about us, so how could it obliterate all traces of Africa? Well, it was said, I think because American and European scholars are very American and very European; that is, they are very ethnocentric; that is, they are very racist. They are more racist than scholarly and they have a very strong and mistaken sense of their own importance and of the validity of their views and interpretations.

There are a variety of ways of trying to reassess our African heritage. One of the more interesting is to read the personal accounts of Africans who lived during that period of our history.

Arna Bontemps collected a series of personal accounts of African enslavement published in the book, *Great Slave Narratives*. One of the most insightful of these was written by Gustavus Vassa, who was born in Benin, West Africa in 1745. When he was about 11 years old, he was captured and sold into slavery. He was brought to America and sold first to a Virginia planatation owner, later to a British naval officer and still later to a merchant in Philadelphia. Subsequently, he was allowed to purchase his freedom and traveled widely as a ship's steward. In 1791 he wrote his autobiography in which he described his childhood and family life in Africa and the manner in which this was disrupted by slavery. He provides one of the most sensitive insights into the kind of historical perspective we need. I have quoted from this work at considerable length in order to encourage the reader to look up the entire story of this remarkable African, and in order to convey both the particulars and the flavor of an important aspect of our African heritage as reflected in his experience. Moreover, these excerpts display Vassa's remarkable command of geography, topography, cultural anthropology, ideas and the English language.

Vassa has described for us the portion of Africa where he was born as follows:

> That part of Africa, known by the name of Guinea, to which the trade for slaves is carried on, extends along the coast above 3400 miles, from Senegal to Angola, and includes a variety of kingdoms. Of these the most considerable is the kingdom of Benin, both as to extent and wealth, the richness and cultivation of the soil, the power of its king, and the number and warlike disposition of the inhabitants. (pp. 4-5)

He was born in rather fortunate circumstances. His father was an elder or chief of his tribe and he was born into a large household where his father had several wives. It should be observed that three distinct patterns of marriage existed in those portions of Africa from which our ancestors came. Under one pattern called polygyny a man had several wives. The number of wives was influenced by the economic and social position of the man as well as the proportion of males and females in the population and the type of economic activity required for family sustenance. A second pattern of marriage called polyandry consisted of situations in which women had more than one husband. Still a third pattern called monogamy involved one wife and one husband. In many parts of Africa, these three patterns of family life existed side by side. In some parts, the most typical situation, patterns of monogamy and polygamy prevailed. In Vassa's own family polygamy was the prevailing pattern.

He has told us also something of the basic pastoral nature of his country and the manner in which this helped to sustain the spirit of community which was another strong feature of our ancestral heritage:

> Our land is uncommonly rich and fruitful, and produces all kinds of vegetables in great abundance. . . . All our industry is exerted to improve these blessings of nature. Agriculture is our chief employment; and everyone, even the children and women, are engaged in it. Thus we are all habituated to labor from our earliest years. Everyone contributes something to the common stock; and, as we are unacquainted with idleness, we have no beggars. (p. 10)

The conditions of the land and the patterns of land utilization, then as now, had an important influence on the social life of the people. Vassa has introduced us to an important aspect of the interaction between the social organization of the family and these basic life conditions.

> The head of the family usually eats alone; his wives and slaves have also their separate tables. Before we taste food we always wash our hands; indeed, our cleanliness on all occasions is extreme, but on this it is an indispensable ceremony. (p. 8)

The influence of the basic conditions of life and the social organization of family and community life are reflected in the more obvious aspects of a people's culture. Vassa continues:

> As our manners are simple, our luxuries are few. The dress of both sexes is nearly the same. It generally consists of a long piece of calico, or muslin, wrapped loosely round the body, somewhat in the form of a highland plaid. This is usually dyed blue, which is our favorite color. It is extracted from a berry, and is brighter and richer than any I have seen in Europe. Besides this, our women of distinction wear golden ornaments, which they dispose with some profusion on their arms and legs. (p. 7)

Furthermore, as we are all aware, we are the inheritors of a most expressive tradition. Vassa has observed:

> We are almost a nation of dancers, musicians, and poets. Thus every great event, such as a triumphant return from battle or other cause of public rejoicing, is celebrated in public dances, which are accompanied with songs and music suited to the occasion.[2] (p. 7)

Still another description of family life in Africa at the time of our ancestors is provided by Venture Smith in a volume of slave narratives edited by John F. Bayliss. Smith tells his own story as follows:

> I was born at Dukandarra, in Guinea, about the year 1729. My father's name was Saungm Furro, Prince of the tribe of Dukandarra. My father had three wives. Polygamy was not uncommon in that country, especially among the rich, as every man was allowed to keep as many wives as he could maintain. By his first wife he had three children. The eldest of them was myself, named by my father, Broteer. The other two were named Cundazo and Soozaduka. My father had two children by his second wife, and one by his third. . . .
>
> The first thing worthy of notice which I remember was, a contention between my father and mother, on account of my father marrying his third wife without the consent of his first and eldest, which was contrary to the custom generally observed among my countrymen. In consequence of this rupture, my mother left her husband and country, and travelled away with her three children to the eastward. I was then five years old. . . .

After relating that his mother left him at the house of a very rich farmer with whom he lived and worked for some time, Smith continues:

> My father sent a man and horse after me. After settling with my guardian for keeping me, he took me away and went for home. It was then about one year since my mother brought me here. Nothing remarkable occurred to us on our journey until we arrived safe home.
>
> I found then that the difference between my parents had been made up previous to their sending for me. On my return, I was received both by my father and mother with great joy and affection, and was once more restored to my paternal dwelling in peace and happiness. I was then about six years old.[3]

These two excerpts of family life in Africa will show something of the patterns of family life among our ancestors. They also show something of the nature of community life and of the problems confronted by our people on the coming of Europeans to that part of Africa.

These excerpts help to illustrate the findings of Professor Chancellor Williams of Howard University in his remarkable new study, *The Destruction of Black Civilization.*[4] He has observed that during the thousand years of African civilizations studied by him there was a series of African kingdoms which rose and flourished and which were destroyed and often rose again. He cites three major factors which help to account for the destruction of those civilizations. One was natural forces which included the expanding desert, pestilence and other natural phenomena. The second factor was the invasion from outside, first on the part of Arabs, then on the part of Europeans. The third major force which accounted for the destruction of these great civilizations was internal bickering and dissension and the lack of unity among the Africans themselves. What Professor Williams points out in his book is that as these civilizations and kingdoms were destroyed, people would often have to disperse and move from one part of Africa to another. New kingdoms arose and even after hundreds of years of being scattered throughout various parts of Africa, there was a strong similarity between the new and the old civilizations. According to his view, this indicates a strong cultural continuity among African people which lasted over hundreds of years so that the values were similar and therefore the new kingdoms were similar in structure to the ones which had been destroyed. In other words, despite the forces of destruction which have been ever present in our experience as African people, there is a strong value base which enables us to put together new civilizations and continue the basic values of our African heritage.

SUGGESTED QUESTIONS FOR STUDY GROUPS

1. Distinguish between the two Africas that Billingsley discusses.
2. How do you account for the differences in opinion of "minority" status among Blacks and Jews?
3. What are some of the implications of our Africaness for our status as American citizens?
4. Identify some of the dominant qualities of our African heritage

which remain with us today. What influence do they have on our life-styles?
5. What were the chief feelings and impressions you had as you read about the life of slave Gustavus Vassa?
6. Identify some of the groups in your community which provide a sense of "somebodyness" for Black people. In what ways do they serve this function?
7. "When we say we are an African people we are not being anti-semitic or anti-white, but we are endeavoring to find the sources of our own strength to build our own communities and our own competence and to strengthen our capacity for contributing to our own governance and our own welfare." Can you think of other illustrations that might help to clarify the basic meaning of the above statement by Billingsley (see page 38)?

3

slavery: the americanization of the africans

When we think of that aspect of our cultural heritage which is American, we are forced to look at the institution of slavery from a Black perspective. It is often said that slavery dehumanized the Africans. Well, when we analyze slavery we must ask ourselves the question, "*Who* became dehumanized in the process?" Or perhaps, as some of my students would say, "Who was inhuman in the first place?" We responded by saying we insist on surviving, and we will do whatever is necessary in order to survive. That's a very human thing. Not only that, we survived that holocaust with a certain sense of, and perhaps because of, a spiritual inclusiveness. We even include other people. We are even willing to live side by side with other people. We are willing to do all sorts of things because of our humanness, which other people have not found it possible to do, at least not graciously. No, we did not become dehumanized by that system. It is accurate to say that the slave system tried to dehumanize us, it tried to crush our humanity, but in the process it exhibited the inhumanity of others and affirmed our humanity because that resilience, that ability to see the reality for what it really is, that capability of bouncing back to live another day is part of our experience. It is part of our history and we ought to be proud, for it has enabled us to survive and make amazing contributions; contributions which the society still does not recognize or appreciate.

All of us have been told that slavery stamped out family life among the slaves; that there was no family life. Now that is not only absolutely untrue, but many Black and even some white scholars are beginning to reanalyze, to look and to see evidences that the strong bonds of family, the strong sense of family that we brought from Africa survived during this slave period. If we see that now, what does it say to us? Does it say that slavery was not really as cruel as we said it was? On the contrary, it says that despite the cruel nature of slavery there was something within us, within our culture and our heritage that enabled us to survive. There was a strong sense of family. There was a strong attachment to family that survived and we, that is to say, our African ancestors, were willing and able to make tremendous sacrifices in order to maintain this sense of family.

There are stories of untold numbers of slaves who were willing, if allowed by their owner, to get up at three o'clock in the morning and walk maybe twenty miles or more to get to the plantation to work in order to meet their responsibilities so as to have the privilege of having a family, and being able to live with their families which were many miles away. It means all sorts of sacrifices were made. It means that we sometimes had to connive and lie; we had to sneak and steal; we had to do all sorts of things in order to maintain a higher value—the spirit of family and community, and we sacrificed for it.

THE IMPACT OF SLAVERY

The impact of slavery on Black family life was devastating; however, it was not fatal. The spirit of family and community bonds brought over from Africa were maintained during this period despite efforts to stamp out all vestiges of family life and African culture. In Volume II of a book, *Key Issues in the Afro-American Experience,* Robert Abzug tells us:

When the war finally ended and all slaves were free, it was not surprising that many made the reuniting of their scattered families the first order of business. "Ask almost any one what they are going to do this winter," a white traveler reported from South Carolina in 1865, "and they will answer you, 'I'se got a sister'—a wife or mother, as the case might be—'in Virginia, and I'm going to look her up and fetch her home." Methods of reuniting families varied. One could place an "Information Wanted" advertisement in the newspapers of localities where the relative might be. Every issue of Negro newspapers during this period usually carried several such plaintive appeals:

INFORMATION WANTED

Of Stephen Harthor, who formerly belonged to Mrs. James Gardiner of this city—was sold in August, 1864, to a gentleman living near Wilmington, N. C. Any information of his whereabouts will be thankfully received by his father at this office.

Ruben Harthor

In places where Negro newspapers did not exist, blacks found other means of reunion, including the arduous method of personal searching. One ex-slave recalled the moment his mother found him after the war. He couldn't believe that it was she: "Then she took the bundle off her hand [sic] and took off her hat, and I saw that scar on her face. Child, look like I had wings." While traveling through the South, a correspondent for the *Nation* came upon a freedman who perhaps had more energy than most. He had walked nearly six hundred miles and had been on the road for almost two months. "[The Negro] had been sold and sent South four years before," explained the newspaperman, "and as soon as he learned he was free, [he was] determined to return to North Carolina and to try to find his wife and children." Those unable or unwilling to make such an effort could only wait and grieve, as did the old slave woman of Poplar Grove, Virginia, who had had twelve children in bondage: "I don't know what has become of one of 'em. It hurts me mightily to think of 'em."[1]

There is something very strong and very resilient in our history which has helped us to survive that we have not yet appreciated.

For it is very clear that the fact that Black people have survived at all in this country is due mainly to the Black family unit and the resilience of the family, and to the spirit of family that exists among us. All that, then, is part of the history that we must somehow recapture and learn ourselves and teach our children, and teach the world.

The manner in which the strong attachment to family survived slavery has been captured in a letter from a Black man to his former slavemaster after a successful escape from slavery. This particular letter as quoted in my book, *Black Families in White America,* was written by Jourdon Anderson:

> Sir: I got your letter, and was glad to find that you had not forgotten Jourdon, and that you wanted me to come back and live with you again, promising to do better for me than anybody else can. . . .
>
> . . . I want to know particularly what the good chance is you propose to give me. I am doing tolerably well here. I get twenty-five dollars a month, with victuals and clothing; have a comfortable home for Mandy,—the folks call her Mrs. Anderson—and the children—Milly, Jane, and Grundy—go to school and are learning well. The teacher says Grundy has a head for a preacher. They go to Sunday School, and Mandy and me attend church regularly. We are kindly treated. Sometimes we overhear others saying, "Them colored people were slaves" down in Tennessee. The children feel hurt when they hear such remarks; but I tell them it was no disgrace in Tennessee to belong to Colonel Anderson. Many darkeys would have been proud, as I used to be, to call you master. Now if you will write and say what wages you will give me, I will be better able to decide whether it would be to my advantage to move back again.
>
> . . . Mandy says she would be afraid to go back without some proof that you were disposed to treat us justly and kindly; and we have concluded to test your sincerity by asking you to send us our wages for the time we served you. This will make us forget and forgive old scores, and rely on your justice and friendship in the future. I served you faithfully for thirty-two years, and Mandy twenty years. At twenty-five dollars a month for me, and two dollars a week for Mandy, our earnings would

amount to eleven thousand six hundred and eighty dollars. Add to this the interest for the time our wages have been kept back, and deduct what you paid for our clothing, and three doctor's visits to me, and pulling a tooth for Mandy, and the balance will show what we are in justice entitled to.

... In answering this letter, please state if there would be any safety for my Milly and Jane, who are now grown up, and both goodlooking girls. You know how it was with poor Matilda and Catherine. I would rather stay here and starve —and die, if it come to that—than have my girls brought to shame by the violence and wickedness of their young masters. You will also please state if there has been any schools opened for the colored children in your neighborhood. The great desire of my life is to give my children an education, and have them form virtuous habits.

Say howdy to George Carter, and thank him for taking the pistol from you when you were shooting at me.[2]

When my research associate and I took a group of my graduate students at Howard University to inspect the Freedmen's Bureau collection in the National Archives, we were introduced to a wealth of data which provides substantial support for the view that slavery, as cruel as it was, was not able to crush the commitment to family life that exists among the Africans.

Our preliminary analysis shows that among 847 couples who had their marriages legalized (registered) in Washington, D. C. at the end of slavery, 490 had been married between 1853 and 1867; 201 between 1843 and 1852; 98 between 1832 and 1842; 29 between 1823 and 1831 and 22 couples had been married before 1823. Furthermore, many of these families could account for their children. Altogether, 139 of these couples could account for 1 child; 170 could account for 2 children; 127 counted 3 children; 79 counted 4 children; 66 counted 5 children; 62 counted 6 children; 33 counted 7 children; 11 counted 8 children, and 26 counted 9 or more children.

A third important finding of this study is that many of the documents present important brief family sketches, such as:

Charles West and Henrietta Chase had their marriage registered in November 1866 by Rev. R. H. Robinson in the District of Columbia. They were married in 1836. They did not state where. They had no marriage ceremony, and the clerk's remarks indicate that they were joined by permission of their master. At the time they registered, they had 9 children.

Andrew Smith and Matilda Miles had their marriage registered in November 1866. They were married in 1826 in Prince Georges County, Maryland by Rev. Mr. Breckingbridge. At the time they registered their marriage, they had 9 children.

Daniel Sanford and Louisa Williams registered their marriage in the District of Columbia in April 1867. Married in 1815 in Fauquier County, Virginia, the Sanfords stated they had 10 children at the time of registry. The clerk's remarks indicated that "Mrs. Sanford is the mother of 21 children. Is still a strong woman."

Isaac Diggs and Letty Smith had their marriage registered in November of 1866. They were married in 1825 in Loudon County, Virginia. The marriage ceremony had been read by their master. At the time of registry they had 11 children.[3]

Thus, despite the impossible conditions of slavery, the Black family survived. Sexual exploitation of slave women by their white owners was widespread. The wide range of color among Black people today is evidence of the white man's exploitation of Black women. Only during the last twenty years of slavery was the number of females equal to that of males. These factors represent massive barriers to the establishment and experience of satisfactory family relationships. Even during slavery, however, there was some social differentiation among the slaves caused principally by their relationship to the slave owners and their place in the division of labor. The three principal groups were the house slaves, the artisans and the field slaves. The house slaves worked in and around the master's house as cooks, nursemaids, butlers and yardmen. The artisans were allowed to develop and practice skilled trades which were needed on the plantations. The field hands planted, cultivated and gathered the crops. The status accrued to the slaves was related to the proximity of their occupation to the house of the master.

In spite of frequent slave uprisings in a vain quest for freedom, the pattern of slavery remained essentially static for over two hundred years. There were, of course, a few Black people who were always free, and a few others who were set free by their masters, or who escaped via the underground railroad. But the bulk of Blacks remained slaves in the rural South until one hundred years ago.

Throughout slavery, since the Black man was not allowed to serve as protector for his family, the Black woman gradually emerged as the most stable, dependable and responsible member of the family. The transition from slavery to emancipation, in addition to its positive consequences, also presented a severe crisis for the Black family. Three patterns of family life emerged from this crisis. First, the majority of Blacks remained on the plantation as tenants of the former owners with little or no wages for their labor.

Second, families which had been allowed to establish common residence and work common plots of ground were often able to maintain their families as social and economic units.

The third pattern was the most disruptive of family life. In those situations where only loose and informal ties had held man and woman together, in spite of the existence of numerous children, these ties were easily severed during the crisis of emancipation. The men tended to join the large bands of homeless men who wandered around the countryside in search of work and new experience.

Women who were thus left behind became further entrenched as the only productive and dependable element in the family. Despite all this, however, the most important untold story of slavery and its aftermath is the story of the resilience of the African heritage which kept the concept of family alive in the culture of Black people, as reflected in the life of Jourdon Anderson and countless other Black people.

SUGGESTED QUESTIONS FOR STUDY GROUPS

1. What impacts did slavery make upon the cultural heritage of Black Americans?
2. How do you account for the inability of slavery—cruel as it was—to eradicate all vestiges of our African heritage?
3. What impact did slavery have on the Black male's family role?
4. How do you respond to Billingsley's assertion: ". . . we sometimes had to connive and lie; we had to sneak and steal; we had

to do all sorts of things in order to maintain a higher value—the spirit of family and community. . . ." (see page 50)?
5. To what extent do you think family unity is a priority among Black families today?
6. Re-read Jourdan Anderson's letter to his former slavemaster (see page 52). What were the dominant emotions you felt as you read it?
7. What were the most significant discoveries you made about slavery as a result of this session?
8. Cite present-day examples which specifically illustrate ways Black families have survived in spite of oppression.

4
teaching our children to walk tall

The very expression, "Walk tall!" is an item of Black culture. It grows out of the fact, the Black fact, that many of us have been able to teach young people to be proud, self-assured, competent, confident and dignified as they go about feeling, being and doing what life requires of them. Reverend Jesse Jackson of People United to Save Humanity (PUSH) has given this Black expression national recognition by using it in his work and speeches to explain the goal of his organization and a major segment of the Black movement. It is tied in with his emphasis on the concept of somebodyness. "I am somebody," he leads his congregation to shout every Saturday morning in Chicago and wherever he goes around the country to give speeches. "I may be poor, on welfare, in jail, persecuted," he shouts, "but I am somebody . . . I'm God's child." Althea Gibson, the Black tennis star, gave currency to this concept a few years ago when she titled her autobiography, *I Always Wanted To Be Somebody*.[1] She made it too.

Sonia Sanchez, the poetess, puts it simply, *We A BaddDDD People*.[2] And forty years before the new Black Revolution, Sterling Brown, a senior faculty member at Howard University, put it even more simply, "strong men," he said, "keep a-comin' on."

It is not easy to teach our children to walk tall. And the fact that so many of us manage to do it so well is further testimony to the resiliency of the human spirit as reflected in our heritage. We have been led by the most urgent of necessities to accomplish the impossible. It has been and continues to be necessary for our people to survive. It has been and continues to be an urgent necessary prerequisite for the survival of our people that we teach our young ones to walk tall in a land which would deny the essence of their very being.

Some people say that it cannot be done. They say that we as a people are too riddled with self-hatred and negative self-concepts to do the job. In fact, for the past twenty years white social scientists have been almost unanimous in describing how we hate ourselves. Only recently have they been challenged by a Black scholar, Nancy L. Arnez who argues with some support from recent research, that the new developments in the Black community have brought to surface a positive conception which we have of ourselves which flies in the face of the previous and still majority findings of low self-esteem and self-hatred among Black people.

It cannot be denied that those who speak of low self-esteem among Black people are touching on an important reality in our communities. One need only think of the harm and hurt we often inflict on each other in a variety of ways on Saturday nights and in the heat of the day as well. But, as Ralph Ellison says, that is only part of the reality of our lives. There is also something else going on, and it is that something else which is the source of our strength, our endurance and our promise as a people. That something else includes an awful lot of love, and hard work, and cooperation, and worship and leadership. Martin Luther King, Jr. knew this, as did Marcus Garvey before him. And that is why they captured our allegiance as a people more than any of our other leaders in this century.

But after all the arguments of scholars and leaders, the task and the burden remains for all of us: How can we teach our children to walk tall, to love themselves and others, to fear no man and to be humble and proud as they strive toward excellence? It is a challenge. God knows it's a challenge. Yet it is an urgent necessity. So, with a great deal of hesitation and a certain amount of trepidation, we advance here some of the suggestions that we, our neighbors, friends and loved ones have found to be helpful in teaching ourselves and our children to walk tall. Some of these suggestions will be individual, others will center in the family, still others in the Black community, and still others must be carried out in the larger society.

THE INDIVIDUAL

As individuals, and particularly, as parents, there are a great many things we can do to fortify the sense of somebodyness in our children. It is my view that children come into the world with an essentially positive predisposition toward themselves and the world. As they grow in consciousness, this develops into a positive conception of themselves. When Black children are very, very young, most of their experiences fortify this positive conception of themselves. I have been a lot of places and seen a lot of families, but it is hard to find a more impressive example of loving care than that of a Black mother for her baby. Or a Black father. Or older sisters and brothers. Or grandparents, friends and neighbors. This is when the child is very, very young. In our communities the child is likely to be showered with love and care no matter who his father or mother is. It is this kind of nurturance which fortifies our children to face the growing-up years and the outside world. The problem for us and our children is, however, that as they grow older, their needs become more complex and their demands more pressing on us. And, as our ability to meet their needs varies, due largely to our own precarious position in this society, the frustrations set in for us and them and negative reinforcements raise their ugly heads in the way we sometimes respond to our children. The task for us, then, is to do the best job we can in the earliest years and to find ways of assisting us in the process as the child grows older.

The best and most lasting means of transmitting to our children a sense of worth, dignity and somebodyness is first to love and accept ourselves as we are. Then, to love and accept the children as they are. That is no easy task, and it is difficult to prescribe exactly how to do it. Yet millions of us accomplish this in a variety of ways. For some, it seems to come naturally. Others have to work at it a bit. For others, it is still more difficult. Some people just seem to despise themselves, and they show this in relationships to their children and others. Some people really think they are no good. Evil. Inadequate. Culturally deprived. Unworthy. Nobody. They show this in how they feel about, talk with or ignore their children. Others just seem able to communicate a sense of worth, dignity and somebodyness to their children by how they play with them, sing to them, show them how to work, go with them to school, take them to church, work, meetings and other important places. They teach them to dance, play, work and to love themselves, their sisters and brothers, parents and others.

ALL IN THE BLACK FAMILY

When we think of things that we might and often do within the context of the family to help instill within our children a sense of who they are, one thinks first of the simple things. We might even call them old-fashioned. For example, my fondest memories of my own childhood include singing with other family members around the fireplace, or in the kitchen, or in the yard, or on trips, or even at work. We sang songs of our heritage—religious songs, spirituals, gospels, work songs. Family singing may be old fashioned, but it is still very popular with young children. The type of songs needs to be carefully selected to appeal to them and to convey part of our heritage as a people. We are a musical people and music is among the more popular means of transmitting our culture. There are few of our great singers today who did not first learn to appreciate music in the family and in the church. Mahalia Jackson, Aretha Franklin, Marvin Gaye, Sarah Vaughn, Della Reese, Lou Rawls and Leontyne Price are among some of the more conspicuous examples. But even for those of us who do not develop into musicians, it helps to develop a positive conception of ourselves.

Not only singing, but dancing within the family is very popular with children. I know that there are still some people whose religious convictions will not allow them to engage in or encourage dancing. Others, however, see dancing as an important means of expression which enables children to think well of themselves, to master something and enjoy it and contribute to the enjoyment of others. Dancing can also be a very educational endeavor when it is done and encouraged consciously and when a wide variety of dances are encouraged and when something of their history or social context is also studied. Surely, Black youth in America are among the world's most creative people and this is nowhere more obvious than in the dance. A friend of mine once said that Black children in any given neighborhood can create a new dance every week, and while the rest of the nation is catching on, they get bored and move on to create others. But what is even more striking is how similar the dances are in every part of the country where Black youth live, and how quickly they seem to pass from one community to another. I was walking down the street one day and saw three little girls skipping rope. I don't know who invented the game, but whoever it was could not have possibly anticipated what those girls would make of it. Rhythm is surely one of our strongest assets as a people. It is unfortunate that it is often others who benefit economically from our talents.

Indoor games can also provide an important vehicle for the development of self-appreciation. When games grow out of, or are consistent with our cultural and social situation, they can be a positive reinforcement for the development of a sense of community. Two new parlor games are favorites in our house. One is "The Afro-American History Mystery Game."[3] It is a table or floor game for two to four players. It consists of a set of four large picture puzzles with important people and events in Black history. The general objective is to be the first to complete your puzzle. The completed puzzles are Joe Louis, Martin Luther King, Jr., the explorer, Matthew Henson and Frederick Douglass. The game is played by spinning a dial, selecting the indicated card and learning the historical facts thus advancing toward the completion of the puzzle. For older children there are a series of 36 additional cards with other facts about other important persons and events in Black history.

A similar game is called "The Black Experience." According to its creators, it is "designed to enhance the awareness of outstanding contributions made by Black Americans to the history of America and the world." This one is played by throwing dice and moving the number of spaces indicated around a board with historical events on it. The objective is to be the first one to "advance from slavery (1619) to the beginning of a new Black Experience."[4]

Books are a major source of child development. Despite television, children still like to read and to be read to, especially in their early years. Our task is to capture their fascination for reading and help them develop a sustained interest in it, and to help expose them to reading material which depicts Black people in a positive light. The greatest number of children's books ignore Black people altogether. Those that include us are often written by white people who have no particular knowledge of our culture or community, and indeed, less interest in us as a people. Consequently, they are likely to be concerned about race relations, that is to say, how white people deal with Black people, which is another way of saying they are mainly concerned about themselves. There is a trickle of books, however, written by Black people which are a genuine joy to behold, and a tremendous aid to us in helping our children move toward self-development, appreciation and competence.

The Drum and Spear Press in Washington, D. C. has put out a series of children's books which are highly recommended. One of them which is most popular is *Children of Africa,* a coloring book for small children which sells for about one dollar. The pictures of African people to be colored are accompanied on the same page by simple text such as "Not too many years ago all the Black children in the world lived in Africa." A somewhat more complex text appears on the opposite page for older readers. These are some examples: "African people controlled their land, the vast continent of Africa, covering more than eleven million miles." Then, toward the middle of the book: "The independence of Africa and her people ended in the 15th century. Africa's people were kidnapped and forceably scattered throughout the world." Then, toward the end: "As parents, we must assume the responsibility of educating our children so that they clearly understand who they are. We are an African people.[5]

Jean Carey Bond, a beautiful and talented Black woman who spent several years in Ghana where her architect husband was working on special assignment, has written two children's books that are among the earliest and finest available. One is, *A is For Africa*.[6] The other, is, *Brown is a Beautiful Color*.[7] Both are generously illustrated with pictures.

When I asked my own children, ages 9 and 10, to list their favorite books on Black people, they gave high priority to two books written by Joyce Cooper Arkhurst, another beautiful and talented Black woman who spent some time in Ghana where her Ghana-born husband was with the foreign service. One is *The Adventures of Spider*,[8] and the second is *More Adventures of Spider*. At this writing the latter sells for less than a dollar. Each book contains six folk tales about the life of a spider. The Introduction to her second book shows the character and purpose of the work:

> All over West Africa, people tell stories about Spider. Most of the stories in this book come from Ghana, a country on the coast of West Africa. They are called "Spider Stories."
>
> When you know the kind of stories people tell, you get some idea of what kind of people they are. You will notice in these stories that West Africans are very particular about three things: Cleanliness, hospitality, and good manners....
>
> Let us begin, then, the telling of our stories. We will start the way storytellers in Ghana often begin to tell a story: "I am the storyteller, and here is my story. Do not believe it, for it never really happened. It is only a story. I am the storyteller, and here is my story."[9]

Also high on my own children's list was *A Quiet Place*, by Rose Blue with pictures by Tom Feelings. This is a series of adventures of a young Black boy named Matthew who is in search of a quiet place to think, read and study. But he is all boy, very ordinary and very appealing. At one point in the book:

> Matthew stayed in his room a long time, lying there staring at the shadows and the cracks in the ceiling, till Baby Stevie woke up and started to cry. Matthew held him and began to feel a little better—holding Stevie made Matthew feel grown-up. When the baby fell asleep again, Matthew put him back in his crib. He was getting pretty hungry, so he left his room and went back into the kitchen.

And, at another point:

> Mama drew Matthew closer and hugged him extra tight and extra long. Then the door slammed and Claudia and Roy came into the kitchen, whispering and laughing.
>
> "Set the table, Claudia," Mama said. "Your papa's still sleeping, so, he'll eat later."
>
> "Right away, Mama, Claudia said. She put her arm around Matthew an said, "Hello, little brother." But Matthew slipped away from her and walked out of the kitchen toward his room because big boys don't cry, at least not when everyone is looking.
>
> "What's the matter, honey?" Claudia started to walk after him, but Roy held her arm.
>
> "Let him be. Sometimes a boy has to be alone and just make the quiet scene."[10]

High on the list, also, is *Luther From the Inner City*,[11] by Brumsic Brandon, Jr. This is a comic strip type characterization of the scenes in the life of a young Black boy and his friends. Still another is *Jackie*,[12] published by Third World Press in Chicago. It is the story of a young Black girl who moves into a new neighborhood. Finally, *I Wish I Had An Afro*,[13] written and photographed by John Shearer, a very promising young, Black photographer.

Then there are the *Golden Legacy*[14] illustrated history magazines which are comic book type histories of prominent Black men and women, including Frederick Douglass and Harriet Tubman. Living in Washington, D. C., near the Eastern Shore of Maryland where both Harriet and Fred grew up, has added to the significance of this aspect of our history for our children. The Frederick Douglass Museum and his home in Anacostia are also important parts of their environment.

Television cartoons are also among the favorites for young children. The national networks have only two which are at all related to the Black experience. One is the Jackson Five cartoon; it is impossible to do anything else in my house on Saturday morning, but watch it. It is sad, however, that despite the fact that the Jackson Five are Black, the world around them in this series is almost always completely white. It is as if the Jackson Five are taken completely out of context. The height of this subtle racism was perhaps the Saturday morning when in the cartoon the Jackson Five went "Back to Indiana." Imagine our distress when in the cartoon, the Jackson Five arrived in Gary to greet the Mayor and the picture showed only the desk and hands of the Mayor. Even then, the Mayor's hands were white. Now, there has never been a white Mayor of Gary, Indiana since the Jackson Five became famous. Indeed, it was Mayor Richard Hatcher, along with the singer, Diana Ross, who helped to make the Jackson Five famous.

Perhaps one of the more enjoyable hours on television, for our purposes here, is "Soul Train." In this program Black youth engage in the kind of dancing which makes the largely white "American Bandstand" seem like a pale imitation of walking. This is also one of the few television programs which has a Black firm among its sponsors. In fact, the commercials done by the Johnson Hair Products Company which makes Afro-Sheen and other products are entertaining and educational in themselves. They are among the most creative and imaginative commercials on television. There is one in which a Black youth is trying to get his Afro together. Suddenly, out of nowhere appears Frederick Douglass who gives him some pointers on how to care for his Afro hairstyle. When Douglass vanishes back into nowhere, the young man yells, "Fred! Fred! Aw, they'll never believe me."

What is most distressing about television programming, in addition to its general decadence, is that the producers and the networks seem to have an absolute aversion to showing the life of representative Black families. Not one national series on Black people presented a complete Black family until the 1973 season. Until then, none of the white or Black oriented programs managed to have a Black husband and wife with children presented on the screen in regular interaction, comic, tragic or otherwise. Even now the programs depicting a regular Black family are often on shows mixed with violence or bigotry. "Good Times," a recent addition, is at the time of writing the single exception.

Of the programs which are national in scope, "Sesame Street" and "The Electric Company" have become perennial favorites with children from 4 through 10 (and older). They show Black people in everyday roles in life, interacting with themselves and with white people on altogether honorable and dignified terms. If these relationships are often a bit contrived and fairytale-like, they are nevertheless altogether positive and constructive as well as entertaining. Also, on the national level, our own children watch "Flip Wilson" regularly. Like a lot of other Black people, they find him entertaining, familiar and altogether absorbing. It is my view that they even see through, enjoy and appreciate the stereotypic behavior represented often by Flip, and are not bothered by it. We, the adults, of course, have some problem with Flip from time to time. We wish he would give a more consistently positive reading of the Black experience, and that he was more consistently masterful and less subservient. But, when all this is said, and when we put Flip up against all the white people on television, we judge him as a positive influence on our efforts to teach our children.

On the national level still, our children were occasionally able to follow "Soul" because of its focus on Black entertainment. They found it difficult to follow "Black Journal" because of its focus on discussion. But they are exposed to these too, for as long as their interest holds. And perhaps equally important, they know that these are regular and highly regarded aspects of their parents' viewing habits.

In Washington, D. C., there are four local television shows with a Black focus, one a daily show and the others weekly, which provide some relief to the otherwise wasteland of television programming. Only one of these is especially designed for children. "The Magic Door" which is hosted by a Black woman, Sheila Thomas, and uses puppets, gives language lessons, plays games and otherwise introduces children to very ordinary aspects of life. While the shows are not consistently Black in content, her own presence and activities give the children a strong sense of identification with her in a most positive way. For our children, however, the most popular local television program is a daily adult series called "Harambee." This is a daily interview show which is very Black in its content and perspective. The host and hostess are Claude Matthews and Carol Randolph, who interview interesting people, mostly Black, on interesting subjects of special interest to the Black community.

There are not many records which portray the Black experience suitably for children. This is a pity, for records are very popular with children. In our house there are some perennial favorites. Ella Jenkins, a young Black woman in Chicago has specialized in recording children's music. She has a number of very fine recordings on the market. They are songs and games for the most part. One children's street song which will be familiar to lots of the readers of this book, goes as follows:

> Oh My!
> I wanna piece of pie
> Well, the pie's too sweet
> I wanna piece of meat
> The meat's too red
> I wanna piece of bread
> The bread's too brown
> I gotta go to town.[15]

Another Jenkins record has a chant which lots of Black children grew up with. It involved clapping hands, slapping palms with a partner, and sometimes adding dance steps:

> Miss May-ree Mack, MACK, MACK
> All dressed in black, BLACK, BLACK
> With silver buttons, BUTTONS, BUTTONS
> All down her back, BACK, BACK.[16]

Then there is another favorite which she does with drums and guitars:

> This train is bound for glory, this train
> This train is bound for glory, this train
> This train is bound for glory
> Children get on board.[17]

One whole album is devoted to "American Negro Folk and Work Song Rhythms," and includes:

> I hear Arch Angels a'rockin' Jerusalem
> I hear Arch Angels a'ringin' dem bells.[18]

Records for children need not be confined, of course, to children's records. "Purlie,"[19] the musical recording, based on

Ossie Davis' play "Purlie Victorious" is high in the estimation of children I know. It helps, of course, if they have the opportunity of seeing the musical itself. And, of course, there are the Jackson Five records. Sometimes, when my girls are in the midst of arguing about which one is going to marry Michael Jackson when they all grow up, I think that if he were to walk through the door they'd both faint standing up. The Edwin Hawkins Singers have the tremendous capacity of making Black people of all ages take note and feel good.

Pictures on the wall are an important feature of many of our homes. Often, however, we miss an opportunity of displaying our own culture and community in this very important way. Some of our homes have all pictures of white people. Children are surrounded by what is considered important. I went recently to a church where all the literature had pictures of white people and there was not a Black picture in the building. I also observed in a recent visit to the music school where my children take piano lessons, that all the pictures on the wall were of white people. Because much of this is the standard daily fare for our children, it is very important for them to be surrounded in their own homes by important people and objects of their own culture. It helps to connect them with important people and events and is another way of sustaining a positive self-concept. In addition, African and Afro-American art is becoming increasingly a part of our lives. In our home the works of Charles White have an honorable place. Other younger artists too, but Charles White is the master. In an introduction to Charles White's book of drawings titled, *Images of Dignity*, Harry Belafonte says,

> There is a powerful, sometimes violent beauty in his artistic interpretation of Negro Americana. . . . The poetic beauty of the Negro idiom . . . is the artist's most profound contribution, . . . it is significant that his art has never strayed far afield from the roots which gave birth to the artist himself."

The late Professor James A. Porter said, "I like to think of Charles White not just as an artist—not even as an American artist, but as an artist who, more than any other, has found a way of embodying in his art the very texture of Negro experience as found in life in America."[20]

It is true still. His boys and girls, men and women are just like us in all our variety and complexity, our joys and our sorrows. A print by Dr. Jeff Donaldson, Chairman of the Art Department at Howard University shows a strong line depicting a father and mother in loving and dignified embrace. This shows the strong continuity between a truly "together" older Black artist and a truly "together" younger one. We are fortunate now that increasing numbers of young artists are doing works which are inexpensive enough that ordinary Black families can afford to hang originals in their homes which help to celebrate our struggle for survival as a people.

IN THE BLACK COMMUNITY

The community which surrounds the family is where much of our children's growing up takes place. The associations, institutions, activities, assistance and obstacles they encounter in the community are an indispensable part of the socialization of our children, that is, they have an indispensable role to play in our ability to teach our children walk tall.

As children grow older and are ready for play groups, nursery school, day care centers, kindergarten, church school, playgrounds and finally school itself, they are subjected to social forces often beyond the control of the family. Two things are important. First, that we give our children a strong fortification of love and positive self-image and competence before they encounter these community forces. Second, that we try to influence these community activities so that they reflect our values and our concerns for our children and our people. Parent participation is only a slogan in most communities and is rarely a reality. This includes the schools. The church is the only major exception and even that often involves parents and children doing separate things at separate times with no major interaction of mutual influence.

I have been discussing what we as individuals and families might do to enhance the development of positive attitudes and behavior in our children. As I approach the closing of this book, may I remind the reader of the importance of the basic theoretical or philosophical position I took in this discussion. I refer to the four levels of social reality within which we all function. These are the individual, the family, the community and the larger society. Furthermore, it is this network of social complexity which makes it difficult for us to "blame" individuals or families for the problems Black people face in this society. At the same time we call attention to the urgent necessity for us to struggle at both the individual and the family level to help fortify our children, ourselves and our communities against the forces of racism and evil and to help encourage ourselves in waging the struggle for survival. For in the final analysis, it is up to us. We should not try to do *all* that needs doing, or to take responsibility for what can best and sometimes only be done by others, but it is our responsibility to set the direction for our own liberation and to preside over its implementation to whatever extent we are able. History certainly teaches us that this process, whether we call it civil rights, racial advancement, Black empowerment, Black liberation or Black nation building, simply cannot be left to others. They will decide in their own interests rather than ours, and history also teaches us that our interests as Black people, growing out of our historical and contemporary situation and predicament, are certainly distinct from the major interests of the dominant group.

Nowhere is the necessity for us to exert our own imprint on the forces which affect our lives more important, apparent and fraught with difficulty than in the area of community institutions. This is true whether we speak of health instructions, education, welfare, religious or any other. The simple fact is that most institutions in our communities do not grow out of our culture, and our own conceptions of our needs. They are designed by others out of their own culture, needs and conceptions and then imposed on us. When they don't work well for us, we are generally blamed. A good example of this is the child welfare system, which I have discussed at some length in a recent book, *Children of the Storm*.[21] Programs of institutional care, child separation from parents, adoption and so on, designed by white people to suit their own needs are foisted off on Black people and when they don't work well, it is said that we are not motivated to help our children, or not qualified to do so. So, the new movement now sweeping the country, that of placing Black babies in white families for adoption, is just another instance where the victims are blamed for their predicament and well meaning, but misguided programs are pursued to the detriment of our children. There is certainly no evidence whatever that white people are able to raise Black children to be Black and beautiful, and proud and competent builders of a civilized world order. There is abundant evidence that they have failed in large measure to do this for their own children.

We are fortunate that the organized Black social work profession has begun a concerted attack on this practice, calling attention to the historic patterns of child care in the Black community, and calling for national programs designed by Black people and supported by national and state governments to provide the necessary financial support and security for Black families to care for these children. The need is urgent, however, for us ordinary people to come to the rescue of these helpless children who are the source of our future as a people.

A similar challenge exists for us in the educational area. We have said above, in several ways, that the family, the church and the school are by far the strongest institutions in the Black community—even today with all the social changes taking place in these and other forms of social life. What is also increasingly clear to us is that the strength, resilience, utility and success of these institutions in accomplishing their mission is directly proportionate to their anchor in Black culture. Thus, the family being insuperably enmeshed in Black culture is the strongest of the three. The church being largely, though not completely independent of white control and contamination is stronger in the accomplishment of its mission than the school. However, the schools in Black communities have been a major source of our strength, our endurance and our promise. Nothing said in this book should take away from that fact. Yet we must, in all candor, admit to ourselves that the schools have fallen far short of effectively educating our people. As Carter G. Woodson informed us as long ago as 1933 in his book, *The Miseducation of the Negro*,[22] the schools have failed largely because they were not designed by or for Black people. They do not reach our children as well as they teach other children because they either ignore or attack the cultural foundations of our children and our communities.

Mrs. Eloise Greenfield, a member of the Black Writers Workshop in Washington, D. C. has written a very attractive children's book which she calls *Bubbles*. In the very first page she takes us inside the experience of a child who is filled with the love of knowledge in the early experiences of school:

> A smile was bubbling inside James Edward on his way home from school, and he opened his lips to let it out. He had learned to read today. He had learned three whole words and he was in a hurry to surprise his Mama and Daddy. A song was bubbling inside him too, and, "I can read songs." But he didn't let it out. He only smiled and kept walking. The three new words were printed on a sheet of paper that was folded and tucked in his pocket. James Edward felt like a lightning bug, warm and glowy, all the way from his inside self to his outside browness.[23]

This is the spirit, the zest for life and for learning that we like to instill and witness in our children. Yet, many of us are painfully aware that this spirit is sapped from our children by the school system and often as they go through school they lose this spirit, in large measure, because the schools are not conceived, designed, administered or taught with an appreciation for the culture and the realities of life for our children.

It is very clear that whatever others may do on our behalf, we must accept the responsibility for defining our situation, developing our own programs, prescribing the role others must play in the process and monitoring the programs and the administration of those programs designed to aid us in the struggle toward liberation as a people and toward self-fulfillment as individuals.

In all this effort, the family is basic. For in the Black community, contrary to what others have written about us, the family is by far the strongest institution we have. It continues to be the primary component of our efforts toward survival and liberation, and it is the key element in our struggle for positive human development. We know that when we think of family in the Black community, we do not confine our thinking—for our experience is not confined—to husband and wife and two children living together in splendid isolation in their own house. We are a more complex and humane people than that. And so the extended family and a multiple variety of nuclear, extended and augmented family forms are an intricate part of what we mean by family. And it must be clear to all of us, as a basis for all we attempt to say and do in the interest of human development, that were it not for the strength, endurance, adaptability and resilience of family life in the Black community, we would not have survived as a people. We cannot, then, allow others to lead us to discard what is most valuable to our own struggle. Nor can we allow the problems we face to obscure our ability to use our strength and our institutions to improve the quality of our lives and strengthen the quality of our demands on the institutional framework of the larger society.

Meanwhile, the struggle for survival must be waged in relation to the following major areas of life as primary foci of our attention, each of which is intricately related to each other:

1. The Black Family
2. A Black Value System
3. Economic System
4. The Educational System
5. The Health System
6. The Communications System
7. The Religious System
8. The Legal System
9. The Neighborhood and Housing System
10. The Recreational System

Each of these systems and their various components must be viewed in dynamic interrelationship with each other. The family, however, is the center. This concept is shown on the following chart (see page 75).

The Black individual, whether child or adult, does not exist in isolation, but is part of family life, whether past, present or future. Similarly, the Black family does not exist as an isolated unit, but is intricately bound up with the Black community and the various institutions, processes, problems and opportunities represented therein. In like manner, the Black community itself is a component of a larger society which must be related to, mastered and transformed in order that Black families function adequately. It is our view that every major legislation at the national, state and local levels ought to be examined by Black elected and appointed officials from the perspective of how that legislation will affect the Black family.

We are particularly concerned that Black children receive, during the first crucial five years of life, the kind of nurture, care, love and physical and emotional support which will fortify them to run the race in later years as they begin to encounter the formal institutions of society.

SUGGESTED QUESTIONS FOR STUDY GROUPS

1. To what extent is the future of the Black child dependent upon what happens in the wider society?
2. How can the Black family prepare the Black child for experiences that he or she will likely encounter in the wider society?
3. What were some of the ways in which your parents prepared you for your venture into the wider society? Do you recall protective measures which your parents used to shield you from exposure to the wider society?
4. Billingsley speaks of the importance of loving and accepting ourselves and our children as both are (see page 59). Illustrate ways in which love and acceptance can be evidenced and communicated.
5. What are some of the factors that contribute to making it difficult for us to teach our children to walk tall?
6. Illustrate ways in which others benefit economically from Black talents.
7. In what ways can community activities be influenced so that they will relfect the values and concerns of Black people?
8. Billingsley writes, "it is our responsibility to set the direction of our own liberation and to preside over its implementation to whatever extent we are able" (see page 70). Why is this such a difficult task? Can you cite instances in which the task has been successfully pursued?
9. Given the ten major areas of life in which the struggle for survival must be waged (see Billingsley, page 73), how would you rank them in terms of importance and priority?
10. Share remembrances and experiences which you had as a child with your parents, adult guardians, relatives and other family neighbors anf friends that gave you a feeling of self-worth; a sense of "somebodyness."

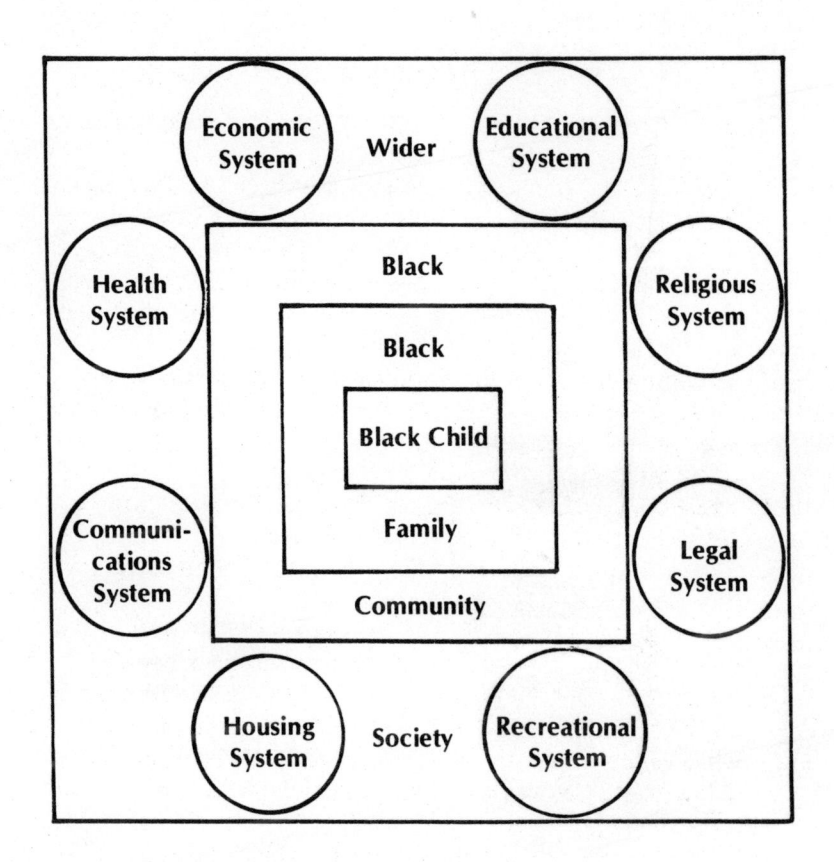

```
┌─────────────────────────────────────────────┐
│      (Economic    Wider   (Educational      │
│       System)             System)           │
│  ┌─────────────────────────────────────┐    │
│ (Health)    │         Black         │  (Religious)│
│ System      │   ┌───────────────┐   │  System │
│             │   │    Black      │   │        │
│             │   │  ┌─────────┐  │   │        │
│             │   │  │Black Child│ │   │        │
│             │   │  └─────────┘  │   │        │
│ (Communi-)  │   │    Family     │   │  (Legal)│
│  cations    │   └───────────────┘   │  System │
│  System     │       Community      │        │
│  └─────────────────────────────────────┘    │
│     (Housing)   Society  (Recreational)     │
│      System              System             │
└─────────────────────────────────────────────┘
```

notes

CHAPTER 1

1. Houston Baker, "Completely Well: One View of Black American Culture," *Key Issues in the Afro-American Experience*, Vol. I, New York: Harcourt Brace Jovanovich, p. 32.
2. Langston Hughes, *Selected Poems*, New York: Alfred A. Knopf, 1959, pp. 8, 13.
3. *Guideposts Magazine: A Practical Guide to Successful Living*, December 1971, pp. 24-26.
4. Andrew Billingsley, *Black Families in White America*, Englewood Cliffs, N.J.: Prentice-Hall, 1968.
5. U.S. Dept. of Commerce, Bureau of the Census, Current Population Reports, Washington, D.C., 1970.
6. Robert Hill, *Strengths of Black Families*, New York: Emerson Hall Publishers, 1971.

CHAPTER 2

1. St. Clair Drake, *The Redemption of Africa and Black Religion,* A Black Paper from the Institute of The Black World, Chicago: Third World Press, 1972, (Introduction by Dr. Vincent Harding, Director, IBW, Atlanta) p. 5.
2. Arna Bontemps, ed., *Great Slave Narratives,* Boston: Beacon Press, 1969, pp. 4-5, 7, 8, 10.
3. John F. Bayliss, ed. *Black Slave Narratives,* New York: Macmillan, 1970, pp. 36, 37, 39.
4. Chancellor Williams, *The Destruction of Black Civilization,* Dubuque, Iowa: Kendal/Hunt Publishing Co., 1971.

CHAPTER 3

1. Robert Abzug, "The Black Family During Reconstruction," in *Key Issues in the Afro-American Experience,* Vol. II, Nathan Huggins, Martin Kilson and Daniel Fox, eds., New York: Harcourt Brace Jovanovich, 1971, pp. 32-33.
2. Billingsley, *Black Families in White America,* pp. 64-65.
3. Marriage Record of the District of Columbia, 1866-67, Asst. Commissioner, Freedmen's Bureau, Record Group 105, National Archives, Washington, D. C.

CHAPTER 4

1. Althea Gibson, ed. by Virginia F. Allen and S. M. Josephs, *I Always Wanted to be Somebody,* New York: Alfred A. Knopf, 1967.
2. Sonia Sanchez, *We a BaddDDD People,* Detroit: Broadside Press, 1970.
3. "The Afro-American History Mystery Game," manufactured by Soular Systems Inc., 1969.
4. "The Black Experience," manufactured by Theme Productions, Inc., Detroit, Michigan, 1971.
5. *Children of Africa: A Coloring Book,* Washington, D. C.: Drum & Spear Press, 1970.
6. Jean Carey Bond, *A is For Africa,* New York: Franklin Watts, Inc., 1969.
7. _____, *Brown is a Beautiful Color,* New York: Franklin Watts, Inc., 1969.

8. Joyce Cooper Arkhurst, *The Adventures of Spider,* New York: Little Brown Co., 1966.
9. _____, *More Adventures of Spider,* New York: Scholastic Book Service, 1972, pp. 5-6.
10. Rose Blue, *A Quiet Place,* New York: Franklin Watts, Inc., 1969, p. 47.
11. Brumsic Brandon, Jr., *Luther From the Inner City,* New York: Paul Erikson, Inc., 1969.
12. Luevester Lewis, *Jackie,* Chicago: Third World Press, 1970.
13. John Shearer, *I Wish I Had An Afro,* NewYork: Cowles Book Co., Inc., 1970.
14. *Golden Legacy: Illustrated History Magazine,* New York: Fitzgerald Publishing Co.
15. Ella Jenkins, "Play Your Instruments and Make a Pretty Sound," Folkways Records, FC 7665, New York, 1968.
16. Ella Jenkins, "You'll Sing a Song and I'll Sing a Song," Folkways Records, FC 7664, New York, 1966.
17. _____, "You'll Sing a Song and I'll Sing a Song," Folkways Records, FC 7664, New York, 1966.
18. "American Negro Folk and Work Song Rhythms," Folkways Records, FC 7654, New York, 1960.
19. "Purlie," based on the play by Ossie Davis, with Cleavon Little, Melba Moore and John Heffernan, Ampex Records, New York.
20. *Images of Dignity: The Drawings of Charles White,* with a Foreword by Harry Belafonte, New York: The Ward Ritchie Press, 1967.
21. Andrew Billingsley and Jeanne Giovannoni, *Children of the Storm: Black Children and American Child Welfare,* New York: Harcourt Brace Jovanovich, 1972.
22. Carter G. Woodson, *The Miseducation of the Negro,* Washington, D. C.: The Associated Publishers, Inc., 1933.
23. Eloise Greenfield, *Bubbles,* Washington, D. C.: Drum & Spear Press. 1972.

study guide

by Robert O. Dulin, Jr. and Edward L. Foggs

A GUIDE FOR GROUP STUDY AND DISCUSSION OF BLACK FAMILIES AND THE STRUGGLE FOR SURVIVAL

The guidance that follows is designed to assist persons in leading young adult and/or parent group discussions based upon the study text *Black Families and the Struggle For Survival*. Through participation in the six, one and a half to two-hour sessions outlined here, group participants are provided an opportunity to become more aware of the continuing role and strategic goal of the Black family. The individual study and group discussion of the ideas explored in this study text will prove extremely helpful to those interested in structuring church ministries in ways that utilize and enhance the strengths of Black family life.

We agree with Andrew Billingsley that "The goal of Black family life is to produce competent individuals, people able to be, to know, to do and above all, to think, to produce competent individuals able to conquer some major aspects of their inner and outer environments in order to survive, to perpetuate the race and make some contributions to the larger society" (see study text 18 and 19).

We also believe the achievement of this goal to be a prerequisite of our survival as Black people.

Since historically the Black church and the Black family continue to be the most viable institutions in the Black community, it is necessary for Black church people, to confront effectively those community issues and other institutions that are capable of either destroying or nurturing Black family life. Therefore, it is our hope that persons using this study text will find it to be a supportive resource for revitalizing the church's ministry with Black families.

Before turning to the session guidance, a word needs to be said in behalf of *group discussion as a learning process*. One of the assumptions of this study guide is that learning can take place through means of group discussion. In this connection, we contend with Flynn and La Faso in their *Group Discussion As Learning Process: A Sourcebook* (New York: Paulist Press, 1972, p. 5) that:

> ... Discussion is a natural human activity ... creative experience.... A shared pursuit of *responsive understanding*—of yourselves, of each other, and of the material under discussion.... it is purposeful conversation among members of a ... group with the assistance of a Leader, based on a Presentation, to develop understanding of a matter of importance, in a *climate* of mutual *trust* and *respect,* with the goals of *community* and *individual decision* and *response.* It is problem-solving in the sense that any learning experience is the seeking of answers to problems of understanding and action.

This definition or understanding of group discussion may cause one to ask: "Who then can be an effective group leader?"

For many persons leading a discussion group proves to be a most difficult task. This task can be made easier if one remembers that it is not necessary for the discussion leader to know more about the subject matter under discussion than anyone else in the group. However, the more he/she knows, the better. But of far greater importance than knowing a lot about the subject matter, is the need for the group leader to be a *real person*. The implies being a person of integrity, one who admonishes honesty and openness. A discussion leader need not shackle himself/herself with a variety of facades and images of phoniness.

In essence, the discussion leader serves the group primarily as a resource person. He/she is, again citing Flynn and LaFaso (p.11), present to *assist group members* in (1) making "a thoughtful examination of the meaning of the material and of the problems it presents," (2) clarifying "their thinking and feeling about problems," and (3) deciding "their individual response."

It is also important for the discussion leader to remember that every member in the group is a potential resource person. It may take considerable time for group participants to consider themselves and each other as resource persons. But with the skillful assistance of an alert discussion leader, members will soon begin to draw upon the unique experiences and insights that each participant has to contribute to the discussion. Thus, one of the major tasks of the discussion leader is to assist others in developing and sharing their own hidden potentials, experiences and insights. This is best done by enabling each participant to feel his or her own value and worth as a person.

One of the ways in which participants are enabled to know themselves as persons of value and worth is through the discussion leader's own recognition and sensitivity to their individual needs and motivations for choosing to be a part of the group and its discussions. The degree to which student needs are met, the degree to which student motivation is recognized and authentically nurtured is the degree to which the discussion leader is said to be successful in facilitating the learning process. Finally, it is by living out his or her personhood, by exhibiting honesty and openness, that the discussion leader is enabled to release the honesty and openness of other group participants. The effective group leader is one who seeks first to be true to oneself in terms of being a real person, and in terms of valuing the personhood of others. When this is done a climate of mutual trust and respect generally prevails. When mutual trust and respect prevail the goals of community, individual decision and response are most effectively achieved. *Alas!* learning takes place.

Getting Started

The first task of all group leaders is to read the entire study text. The more familiar you are with the subject matter to be discussed,

the easier it will be for you to function as a discussion leader. However, you should not satisfy yourself with this <u>one</u> reading of the study text. As the session guidance will indicate, <u>you are encouraged to re-read</u> various sections of the study text and in some cases other resources—for purposes of more adequately familiarizing yourself with the subject matter to be discussed.

It may be that you have already organized a young adult or parent study group. If so, the use of this text may be one in a series of topics being considered by members of your group. If not, you may want to take this opportunity to form such a group.

If you are forming a new group, your first session could be arranged by sending a letter of invitation informing parents or other young adults of this six-session study and discussion group that will convene on (*state the dates you plan to meet, time, and where you will be meeting*). This initial letter should be followed with announcements, phone calls and other personal contacts encouraging those invited to participate in this learning experience. You may also want to encourage those invited to make themselves a committee of one, or two if a couple, responsible for bringing another person or couple to share with them in these scheduled sessions.

Should it prove necessary for you to charge an admission fee for persons attending these small group discussions, this should also be mentioned in your letter of invitation. These monies could be used to purchase refreshments for serving during the various sessions, as well as purchasing copies of this study book for each participating member. Charging a small admission fee may also result in a more definite *committment to regular attendance* on the part of those who may decide to share in these discussion sessions.

Session I: Ideas and Patterns of Black Family Life

Leader's Preparation. Read page 11 to "The Role of Women in the Family and in the Community" on page 29 of Chapter I.

Goal: To explore ways in which Black family life is involved in culture and community, and to discover and list viable goals for Black family life.

Materials Needed.

1. A copy of the study text *Black Families and the Struggle For Survival* by Andrew Billingsley for each group member.

2. The four "basic ideas" and small group tasks as indicated in Step 4 of the "Leader's Function in Session" below. Each basic idea and task should be typed or written on a separate sheet of paper, or on a 5 x 8 note card.

Leader's Function in Session.

1. If this is a new group being formed, or if there are several new persons in your group, take ten to twelve minutes for engaging in some creative get acquainted exercise. Making light refreshments available and encouraging persons to mingle, meeting as many new persons as possible, is one means of getting acquainted. This tends also to encourage relaxation. It helps to create a feeling of groupness on the part of individual members.

2. An interesting, exciting and creative orientation period may mean the difference between retaining or losing members from future sessions. Therefore, a distribution of the study text (i.e. one copy for each group member), a brief survey of its contents, a general review of the session goals and of what may be expected from this session and those to follow should be a first step in the emotional preparation of persons for participation in these planned group discussions and learning experiences.

3. Using newsprint, chalkboard, overhead projector or some other visual aid, take twenty minutes to present the four basic ideas outlined by Billingsley as being crucial to a "discussion of Black families and their contribution to the struggle of Black people for survival, meaning and achievement." Your presentation should illustrate, as does Billingsley's thought, specific ways in which these four basic ideas are related to Black family life. For example, Billingsley lists one of these basic ideas as being *Black culture.* For dramatic effect and for purposes of holding the attention of group members, an outline, such as the following one in bold type could be written on newsprint. This could be done for each of the basic ideas. It should be done before the session begins, so as not to take up time during the session for writing this or other illustrative outlines that may serve to facilitate a coherent and exciting presentation. The other basic ideas are *Black consciousness, Black community* and *Black competence.*

BLACK CULTURE

... the role of the Black family in the struggle for survival ...

1. ... the repository for the culture of our people ...

2. ... the intimate setting in which the Black woman continues to be the major creator, transmitter and repository of our cultural heritage, etc. ...

3. ... the protector and inspirer of the Black child ...

4. Take fifteen minutes to entertain any *clarifying questions*. If there are no questions, or at the end of fifteen minutes, divide into four smaller groups. Distribute to each group one of the basic ideas listed in the following copy. Have each group discuss the idea it has been given in terms of the question or task indicated. Each of these ideas and task should be typed or written on a separate sheet of paper prior to the beginning of this first session, in order that they might be given quickly to each small group. This will enable each group to focus immediately upon its own task.

BLACK CULTURE:
Have one person in your group to read aloud that section of the study text regarding BLACK CULTURE, beginning with the sentence "In contemporary discussions," on page 14 and reading through to the second basic idea on page 17. When finished, discuss as a group the distinctive characteristics of Black culture as observed by Billingsley, and share any other illustrations that indicate ways in which Black people are a distinct people. Using newsprint list these along with the distinctives observed by Billingsley.

BLACK CONSCIOUSNESS:
Have one person in your group read aloud that section of the study text regarding BLACK CONSCIOUSNESS. When finished, illustrate and discuss as a group specific ways in which the Black family and the Black church have kept alive the Black consciousness of Black people. In a brief, but precise manner list your specific illustrations on newsprint. List also other ways in which the Black family and the Black church might function so as to keep alive our Black consciousness.

BLACK COMMUNITY:
Have one person in your group read aloud that section of the study text regarding BLACK COMMUNITY. When finished, illustrate and discuss as a group specific ways in which the joint functioning of the Black family and the Black church have served to confirm the sense that we (i.e. Black people), are somebody. List your illustrations on newsprint along with any other suggested ways in which this sense of "somebodyness" might be enhanced through Black family life or Black church ministries.

BLACK COMPETENCE:
Have one person in your group read aloud that section of the study text regarding BLACK COMPETENCE (i.e. pages 18-19). When finished, illustrate and discuss as a group ways in which the Black family and the Black church have contributed to developing a sense of competence in the young. List on newsprint these and other ways in which the Black family and Black church might continue to contribute to developing a sense of competence in children and youth.

5. Sharing as a total group, have one representative from each of the smaller groups to state their group task and, using their group's newsprint listings, the specific ways in which their group responded to its task. Allow about five to six minutes for each group's report.

6. As discussion leader, close this session by reviewing some of the more viable goals for Black family life. Your comments should include those goals listed by Billingsley on pages 18 and 19 of the study text. Any summary statements made will be more relevant to the session discussions if attention is called to some of the newsprint listings as possible ways of achieving these stated goals for Black family life.

Preparation for Next Session.

1. All group members should read Chapter I, "Black Families in Perspective."

2. Ask participants to bring to Session II a brief, clearly written and complete statement concerning one *new idea* which they have discovered as a result of reading Chapter I.

Session II: The Role of Women in the Family and in the Community

Leader's Preparation. Read "The Role of Women in the Family and in the Community;" pages 29 to 34 of Chapter I. If a greater understanding of the role and meaning of the Black woman and of Black womanhood in the family and in the community is desired, refer to: "Tomorrow's Tomorrow: The Black Woman" by Joyce A. Ladner, 1972, Doubleday, $1.95. "Silent Voices" by Josephine Carson, 1969, Delacorte Press. $2.95. "Black Woman in America" by Robert Staples, 1973, Nelson-Hall, $8.95. These are available from your local library or bookstore. "The Black Scholar: Journal of Black Studies and Research," Volume 3, Number 4, December 1971; and also Volume 4, Numbers 6-9, March—April 1973 are extremely helpful publications focusing upon the Black woman and Black women's liberation. These are available in your local library, or by writing The Black World Foundation, P. O. Box 908, Sausalito, California 94965. Single copies sell for $1.25.

Those wanting more information concerning Black aging and the aged Black should consult "The Multiple Hazards of Age and Race: The Situation of Aged Blacks in the United States." This is a report by the special Committee on Aging, United States Senate and is available for 35¢ from the Superintendent of Documents, U. S. Government Printing Office, Washington, D. C. 20402.

Goal. To share personal experiences and insights that illustrate ways in which culture and other forces contribute to the development of various competencies among Black people, and to provide opportunity for participants to celebrate Black womanhood.

Materials Needed. Guidance for this session suggests the use of a motion picture film or sound filmstrip concerning the Black woman and/or Black womanhood. We recommend use of the filmstrip "Womanhood" from the 6-color sound filmstrip set *Black Poems, Black Images,* available from Warren Schloat Productions, Inc., Pleasantville, New York 10570. When ordering request price quotation for individual items and use catalogue No. S/323. For other films or filmstrips regarding Black womanhood consult your local film library or nearest film distributor. To add flair and to help set the mood for this session decorate the walls of your meeting room with the names and/or picture-posters of outstanding Black women.

In order to personalize the goal for this session, include in your wall-posters the names and/or pictures of Black women from your own church, club, community, etc.

Leader's Function in Session.

1. After stating the goal and purpose of this session, have participants take the written statements concerning the one *new thing learned* from reading Chapter I of the study text and hold it so that it can be read easily as group members mingle reading as many of each other's statements as possible. Persons should feel free to discuss or clarify among themselves any statements read.

2. In groups of 4 or 5, discuss any feelings or insights gained regarding the unique lives of those Black persons discussed on pages 19 to 29 of the study text. Then share personal experiences or knowledge of personal acquaintances or relatives whose lives illustrate ways in which culture and other forces have contributed to the development of their various competencies. Each group should select from its discussions the one *personal story or experience* regarding an outstanding Black woman whose path to competency reflects best Billingsley's concept of "screens of opportunity." The story selected is to be shared with the total group.

3. As a total group, have one representative from each of the small groups to share their group's choice of the personal story that illustrates Billingsley's concept of "screens of opportunity."

4. Close this session by showing the sound filmstrip "Womanhood," or some other film of your choice related to Black womanhood. Your choice of a film should probably not last longer than twenty or twenty-five minutes.

Preparation for Next Session.

1. Have group members read Chapter II, "We are an African People."

2. Call attention to any TV presentations focusing on African heritage or Black history which may happen to be scheduled in your area between now and the next session. Consult your *TV Guide* or, for more advanced listings see *Cultural Information Service* (P. O. Box 92, New York, NY 10016). CIS is published monthly, 11 times a year (combined July-August issue). Annual subscription, $12. Single copy. $1.25.

Session III: We Are An African People

Leader's Preparation.

1. Read Chapter II, "We Are An African People."
2. Secure a large world map that can be wall mounted. Be prepared to assist the group in identifying the seven major concentrations of African peoples throughout the world. You may want to use color-coded adhesive dots to represent the various areas.
3. Additional helpful illustrated material on African heritage may be found in the pamphlet series, *African History*, by Earl Sweeting. Available from the African-American International Press, P. O. Box 775, Flushing, N.Y. 11352.
4. You might invite a native African (perhaps a student) to visit this session to discuss and compare family life today on the African continent with Black family life in the United States.
5. You could arrange a field experience between sessions three and four for the group to visit one or two community groups which give unique expression to our Africaness.

Goal. To aid the group in developing a fuller awareness and appreciation of our African heritage and a positive understanding of its beneficial influences upon Americans of African descent.

Materials Needed for Session.

1. Large world map
2. Colored adhesive dots
3. Tape or other means of mounting wall map
4. Refreshments, if desired

Leader's Function in Session.

1. Have group identify on the world map areas of major concentrations of African peoples.
2. Have several groups of four or five each to select one major current issue and discuss ways in which our Africaness influences how we look at these issues and how Black families are affected by these issues. Issues could include such matters as an upcoming election, a local community controversy, the local use of revenue sharing money, crisis situations, recent or proposed actions of governmental bodies, police-community relations, etc. The smaller groups should then reconvene (after thirty to thirty-five minutes) and share insights gained. Particular attention should be given to common threads that run through the varied issues.

3. Lead the group in exploring some of the questions at the end of Chapter II.

Preparation for Next Session.

1. Assign the group to read Chapter III, "Slavery: The Americanization of the Africans."

2. Have some members of the group to plan to share additional personal accounts of African enslavement selected from Arna Bontemp's book, *Great Slave Narratives.*

Session IV: Slavery: The Americanization of the Africans

Leader's Preparation.

1. In addition to reading Chapter III, "Slavery: The Americanization of the Africans," secure a personal or library copy of *The Negro American: A Documentary History* by Leslie H. Fishel, Jr. and Benjamin Quarles (Glenview, Illinois: Scott, Foresman and Co., 1967). Selected readings from this source can serve to supplement the slave narrative accounts quoted by Billingsley.

2. Check with your local public library or a nearby campus for possible films dealing with slavery and Black history.

3. Inquire to see if there might be a person in your community whose parents or grandparents were enslaved. Such persons should be an invaluable resource for this session. You might arrange for a panel of members from the group to interview this person. It would add some vital, firsthand information.

Goal. To enable the group to gain meaningful perspectives on the influences of slavery on the cultural heritage of Black Americans, particularly Black families, and to inspire continuing loyalty to the strengths that Black families have nurtured amid adversity.

Materials Needed for Session. If you use a film, be sure to arrange in advance for projector, screen, projectionist and extra projector bulb.

Leader's Function in Session.

1. Simulate (role play) a family setting and have the family attempt to resolve a pressing problem or need. The rest of the group should be observers at first and then react later to the attempt to resolve the problem in terms of what influences they saw at work as the family wrestled with their situation.

2. Using current census data, examine the circumstances of

Black families in your community. Information such as population distribution, housing conditions, income and educational levels, etc. may be prepared on a chart for group discussion. Try to determine the extent to which your community's conditions still reflect vestiges of the influence of slavery. Your city or county planning body, area Census Bureau office or the Superintendent of Documents, Washington, D. C. 20402, can supply you with publications containing population data for your city, usually at nominal cost.

3. As further attention is given to the slave narratives, or an interview with a former slave, focus upon the positive qualities of an enslaved people. Consider what bearing these qualities had on the crisis of emancipation.

Preparation for Next Session.

1. Chapter IV, "Teaching Our Children to Walk Tall," should be read by the group, with particular attention to the systems chart on page 75.

2. Discuss with members of your family some of the ideas in Chapter IV. Be prepared to share some of their responses and reactions in the larger group session.

Session V. Teaching Our Children to Walk Tall

Leader's Preparation.

1. Read carefully Chapter IV, "Teaching Our Children to Walk Tall," noting especially the variety of resources highlighted in this chapter.

2. Prepare an exercise copy of the systems chart on page 75, without the circles. Duplicate enough copies for the entire group. See further instructions, *Leader's Function in Session.*

3. Be prepared to lead group in other experiences outlined under

Leader's Function in Session.

Goal. To provide an opportunity for the group to discover some of the concrete means that Black families can utilize in teaching their children to walk tall, to love themselves and others and to strive toward excellence.

Materials Needed for Session.

1. Systems chart
2. Pencils and rulers

Leader's Function in Session.

1. Given Billingsley's emphasis on the three primary institutions that exert key influence on the development of the Black child, participants in the session might be arranged in three groupings discussing the relative importance of family, church and school on the growing Black child. Consider where their roles overlap and in what respects they are distinct and unique. Help the group to explore concrete steps they can take toward strengthening these institutions in the community.

2. Have all persons indicate on the systems chart those systems in the wider society which they are most consciously aware of having shaped and influenced their lives from childhood. This may be indicated by the size of the circle one draws around a given system and with lines extending from the center box (Black Child) to the appropriate circle. The larger the circle, the greater the influence. After all have finished, encourage the group to circulate the charts among themselves. Be alert to any significant differences in influences noted. Do they seem to center around age, characteristics of area such as rural or urban or other notable factors? Are there influences cited which are not adequately covered by any of these systems?

Preparation for Next Session.

1. The next session is designed to provide exposure and use of many of the resources cited in Chapter IV. It will be a kind of gala fun time as well as a learning/sharing experience, and should offer excitement for all. You won't want to miss it!

2. Since it is the final session of this series, it may be helpful to reflect upon the earlier sessions with a view toward appropriating the insights and understandings gained thus far through the various media and resources that will be shared.

3. Bring a few extra coins with you since some materials will be available for you to purchase.

Session VI: *(Special Session):* **Family Fun Council for Teaching Our Children to Walk Tall**

Leader's Preparation. Planning and preparation for this session *should begin early.* Your greatest preparatory task will be to secure at least six other leaders to work with you in planning and implementing this session. Among the six selected one should be skilled in music, able to play the piano and teach new *songs for family singing;* another should be prepared to teach persons *how to play* various family games; another should be capable of reading, reviewing and selling children's records; another, with running a 16-millimeter film projector and setting up a Black arts display. A sixth person should be responsible for preparing and serving light refreshments. More about these leader's tasks and responsibilities are outlined below under "Leader's Function In Session."

As you become familiar with these responsibilities, you may discover that some of them might be carried out more effectively and creatively by a family unit acting as leader, rather than by one individual acting as leader. The nature of some of the program responsibilities, etc., might also suggest that you secure the services of outside resource persons—or family units—who may be more proficient in the five areas identified above. In essence, your ultimate goal *is to work with these selected leaders in planning and implementing a Family Fun Council For Teaching Our Children To Walk Tall.* The concept, structure and process of a Family Fun Council for Teaching Our Children to Walk Tall is centered in a series of booths, or preferably separate rooms, each staffed and supplied with the appropriate resources and display materials necessary for each of the five selected leaders to carry out their responsibilities in relation to:

Room 1: INDOOR FAMILY GAMES
Room 2: CHILDREN'S MAGAZINES AND BOOK-A-RAMA
Room 3: CHILDREN'S STORY AND MUSICAL RECORDS
Room 4: SONGS FOR FAMILY SINGING
Room 5: BLACK ARTS AND CRAFTS

The session process should move along so as to allow group members the opportunity to spend twenty minutes exploring the resources, listening, learning, sharing and discussing ideas available in each of the five rooms. Depending upon the size of your study group, you may choose (1) to move from room to room as a total group. Or you may choose (2) to form five smaller groups and rotate in a way that allows each small group the opportunity to spend twenty minutes in each room. The latter process will necessitate that each group leader do a repeat performance and/or presentation for each new group. In either case you will want to devise some means of informing leaders when twenty minutes have elapsed signaling group member's movement to another room. In the interest of time, movement from room to room should be done as quickly as possible. This entire process will take about one hour and forty-five minutes.

Goal. To provide opportunity for fun and fellowship and for parents and other interested adults to become more familiar with the literary and musical resources, family games, etc., available for use in "teaching our children to walk tall."

Materials Needed.

1. Refreshments (hot and/or cold drinks, party sandwiches, cookies, etc).

2. Room 1: Indoor family games, books* etc. on display and for sale about ideas for indoor games.

3. Room 2: A wide variety of children's books* on display and for sale. Books for parents about parent-child relationships, child rearing, etc., should also constitute a part of your BOOK-A-RAMA. For example, *The Black Child: A Parents' Guide* by Phyllis Harrison-Ross, M.D., and Barbara Wyden is one of the resources with which Black parents will want to familiarize themselves. Published by Peter H. Wyden, Inc., 750 Third Ave., New York, N.Y. 10017, the book is available for $7.95. Display also various children's magazines. You may want to contact the proper sources and make some arrangements for securing subscriptions from group members to various children's magazines. For example, Johnson Publishing Co. Inc., at 820 South Michigan Avenue, Chicago, Illinois 60605, now publishes an *Ebony, Jr.* Check your local library for other relevant children's magazines.

4. Room 3: A good record player. Secure from your local library or record distributor a wide variety of songs and musical records* for display and listening purposes.

5. Room 4: A piano, relevant children's song books* on display

---

*PLEASE NOTE. Most retail bookstores and book distributors have policies and consignment programs for making a wide assortment of books and other literature available to civic and church groups.

and for sale, mimeographed songs for distribution and use in teaching new songs.

6. Room 5: A 16-millimeter film projector and screen. The 16-millimeter film *Arts and Crafts of West Africa,* 10 minutes, color, 1969. A Wayne Mitchell Film. Available from BFA Educational Media, a division of Columbia Broadcasting System, Inc. (Bailey —Film Associates), 2211 Michigan Ave. Santa Monica, California 90404. Write for rental information. This film explores a variety of West Africa's art forms—sculpture, metal work, cloth dying, building ornamentation, carving, etc. Highly recommended for use with primary through adult groups. Scout around in your community for Black artists who may assist you in arranging a Black arts and crafts display. Arrangements might also be made for selling to group members various art pieces on display.

Leader's Function in Session.

1. As over all group leader, your major responsibility will be that of program coordinator. At a designated hour, when the total group is assembled, state the purpose and process to be followed in this session. Allow about one hour and forty-five minutes to complete the room-to-room phase of the session. It is the responsibility of your other group leaders to involve persons in the various listening and learning activities, etc. that relate to their room's specific area of concern. For example, in:

Room 1 group members are to be involved in ways that acquaint them with various indoor family games.

• Room 1 group members are to be involved in ways that acquaint them with various indoor family games.

• Room 2 group members should hear a brief review of one or two select books, have opportunity for browsing, asking questions, making purchases, etc.

• Room 3 should provide group members opportunity to hear various children's story and musical records.

A mini-lecture could be given on the *educational values of children's records,* etc. Entertain any questions.

• Room 4 persons should be introduced to the fun and values of family singing. Opportunity should be provided for learning relevant family songs.

• Room 5 the ten-minute film *Arts and Crafts of West Africa* should be shown. Members should then have opportunity to browse through the art display. If local artists are available, group members may want to share in conversation with them, or make purchases of various art pieces. If purchases are made, they should not be taken from the display area until the close of this session. This will allow group members an opportunity to see the complete art display.

2. Refreshments should be made available at this time. Group members should also be free to spend another twenty minutes in the room or rooms of their choice, at the end you should announce the close of this session.

301.42 Billingsley, Andrew
Bil

Black Families and the
Struggle for
Survival

DATE DUE

CHICAGO BLACK METHODISTS FOR CHURCH RENEWAL
1240 EAST 79th STREET
CHICAGO, ILLINOIS 60619